TOP
SECRET
FILES

WORLD
WAR I

TOP SECRET FILES

WORLD WAR I

STEPHANIE BEARCE

PRUFROCK PRESS INC.
WACO, TEXAS

Library of Congress Cataloging-in-Publication Data

Bearce, Stephanie.
  Top secret files : World War I spies, secret missions, and hidden facts from World War
I / by Stephanie Bearce.
    pages cm
  ISBN 978-1-61821-241-2 (pbk.)
  1.   World War, 1914-1918--Secret service--Juvenile literature. 2.   World War,
1914-1918--Underground movements--Juvenile literature. 3. Spies--History--20th cen-
tury--Juvenile literature. I. Title. II. Title: World War I spies, secret missions, and hidden
facts from World War I.
  D639.S7B335 2014
  940.3'1--dc23
                                2014028292

Copyright ©2015 Prufrock Press Inc.

Edited by Lacy Compton

Cover and layout design by Raquel Trevino

Background cover image courtesy of the Missouri Division of Tourism

Illustrations by Zachary Hamby on pages 11, 14, 16, 22, 28–29, 30, 32–33, 39–40, and 52

ISBN-13: 978-1-61821-241-2

No part of this book may be reproduced, translated, stored in a retrieval system, or trans-
mitted, in any form or by any means, electronic, mechanical, photocopying, microfilm-
ing, recording, or otherwise, without written permission from the publisher.

Printed in the United States of America.

At the time of this book's publication, all facts and figures cited are the most current
available. All telephone numbers, addresses, and website URLs are accurate and active.
All publications, organizations, websites, and other resources exist as described in the
book, and all have been verified. The author and Prufrock Press Inc. make no warranty
or guarantee concerning the information and materials given out by organizations or
content found at websites, and we are not responsible for any changes that occur after
this book's publication. If you find an error, please contact Prufrock Press Inc.

Prufrock Press Inc.
P.O. Box 8813
Waco, TX 76714-8813
Phone: (800) 998-2208
Fax: (800) 240-0333
http://www.prufrock.com

TABLE OF CONTENTS

SECRET WEAPONS

SECRET FORCES

SECRETS

THE BLACK HAND

Black Hand seal

Can a war really start because of a secret society? World War I did. It all began with a secret society called the Black Hand. In 1911, the country of Serbia was under the rule of Austria-Hungary. Many Serbians did not like this and wanted to govern their own land, so a few members of the Serbian Army formed an undercover operation called the Black Hand. This undercover operation was designed to free Serbia from the control of Austria-Hungary.

Every member took a vow of freedom or death, and all members promised to follow the orders of their commanders without asking questions. The Black Hand society was so secretive that members were not even allowed to know the names of associates outside their own local group.

Archduke Franz Ferdinand of Austria, 1919

Their plan was simple and deadly. They would assassinate the heir of the Emperor of Austria. Members of the Black Hand believed killing Archduke Franz Ferdinand would be just revenge for Austria-Hungary taking over the rule of Serbia. They hoped that killing him would lead to freedom for Serbia.

Spies of the Black Hand learned that Archduke Ferdinand and his wife Sophie were scheduled to inspect the troops in Sarajevo, Bosnia, during June of 1914. The leaders of the Black Hand decided this would be the best time to put their plan into action. Three trainees were selected for the job and secretly snuck into Sarajevo a month before the Archduke's visit. Three more spies of the Black Hand joined the group and came armed with four army pistols and six bombs.

Security for the June visit was not high. The Archduke was brave and didn't like having too many secret service men following him. He also liked to be near the people he ruled and didn't want to be blocked from the crowd by the military. For the most part, the Bosnians were excited to have the Archduke visit and most people did not think there would be any problems during the trip.

Archduke Ferdinand and his wife, Sophie, rode through the streets of Sarajevo in a convertible waving to the crowds of onlookers. Hundreds of people lined the streets to cheer and welcome the royal couple. Among those cheering people were the assassins from the Black Hand. The young men spread themselves out among the crowd. As the cars passed the first assassin, he lost his nerve and did nothing. The second assassin had more resolve, took a bomb from his coat pocket, lit it, and threw it at Archduke Ferdinand.

The bomb bounced off the back of the car and into the crowd. The explosion rocked the ground and injured about a dozen people. The car behind the Archduke was hit with shrapnel and injured the Archduke's friend, Lieutenant Colonel Merizzi. Hearing the explosion, the Archduke's driver sped away from the bomb scene and got the Archduke and his wife to safety.

A QUICK WAR?

When WWI initially began in July of 1914, many believed it would be over quickly. Various accounts have both sides of the war stating it would end shortly, with Kaiser Wilhelm II, the German Emperor, telling his troops they would be "home before the leaves have fallen from the trees," and Germany only stockpiling enough potassium nitrate (used for gunpowder) for 6 months. Needless to say, their estimates were wrong, as the war did not officially end until November 11, 1918.

The Black Hand assassin tried to follow the rules of his secret society by swallowing a cyanide poison pill and jumping into the river. Little did he know, the poison was old and the river was only a few inches deep. The pill made him vomit, and the crowd captured him and turned him over to the police.

The Archduke and his wife had escaped unharmed. Later that day, the couple decided to visit their friend, Lieutenant Colonel Merizzi in the hospital. Unfortunately, the car drivers were not told of the change in plans. That would have been Merizzi's job. The drivers continued on the planned route and the other assassins were still waiting.

As the Archduke's car drove down Franz Joseph Street, another Black Hand assassin took aim. This time, the weapon was a gun. Two shots were fired into the car, striking the Archduke in the neck and his wife in the abdomen. Both died.

Austria-Hungary knew nothing of the secretive Black Hand society and blamed the Serbian government for the deaths of Archduke Ferdinand and Sophie. It declared war on Serbia. Russia had made treaties that promised they would support Serbia in a war so it declared war on Austria-Hungary. Germany sided with Austria-Hungary, and France supported Russia. Germany then invaded Belgium on its way to France. Britain had guaranteed to defend Belgium against invaders so Britain declared war on Germany. Just 30 days after the Archduke and his wife were killed, The Great War had begun. And it was all because of a secret society called the Black Hand.

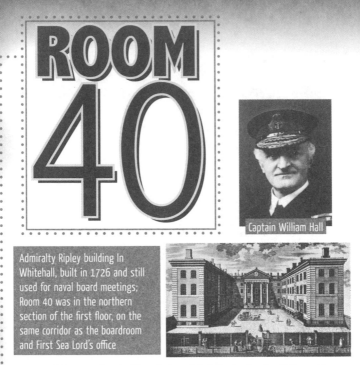

ROOM 40

Captain William Hall

Admiralty Ripley building In Whitehall, built in 1726 and still used for naval board meetings; Room 40 was in the northern section of the first floor, on the same corridor as the boardroom and First Sea Lord's office

Hidden in the halls of the old Admiralty building, Room 40 didn't look like anything special. But behind the locked door, British code breakers were working feverishly to decode German military messages.

The men and women who reported to Room 40 were not typical soldiers or military types. They were scholars, professors, amateur puzzle solvers, and telegraph operators. The one thing they had in common was an innate ability to solve puzzles and understand codes.

The operations in the room were so secret that code breakers had to hide their work when visitors came into the room. Sometimes the code breakers themselves had to go hide in the secretary's office so no one would know who was working in the room.

The leader of Room 40 was Captain William Hall. Nicknamed Blinker because of a facial tick, he understood how important it was for the Allies to intercept and understand the codes of Germany and the Central Powers. If the Allies could break the codes and not let Germany know the codes were broken, then Germany would continue to send messages for the Allies to intercept. The Allies would know the exact locations of the German ships.

The team in Room 40 benefitted from the Russian discovery of two German Navy codebooks. The Russians kept one for their own use but passed one along to the British. The codebook enabled the team to make great strides in understanding German messages.

For example, Room 40 was able to warn the British Navy when the Germans were headed out to the North Sea and sent ships to intercept them. They also decoded the famous Zimmermann telegram that helped convince the United States to declare war on Germany.

During the war, Room 40 decrypted more than 15,000 German communications. They worked with all forms of communication from letters and telegraph to wireless communications. German radio transmissions were intercepted at locations such as the Coastguard station at Hunstanton in Norfolk and passed on to the code breakers of Room 40 for decrypting.

The work of the people in Room 40 was incredibly valuable to the war effort, but the staff of Room 40 was not recognized for their service until decades after the end of the war. Their work was considered top secret and files were not released until the 1980s!

Splish Splash!

Dilly Knox was known as one of the best code breakers in Room 40. He claimed he did his best work in the bathtub. To help him work, a bathtub was installed in Room 53 down the hall from Room 40.

THE ZIMMERMANN TELEGRAM

Woodrow Wilson, President of the
United States of America, 1919

War had been raging across Europe since
1914, but for 2 years, President Woodrow
Wilson had counseled the American public
to remain neutral. Americans did not want
to get involved in a war far across the
ocean, and they re-elected Wilson in 1916
with the slogan "He kept us out of war."

It wasn't easy for Wilson to convince everyone that they should not help out their European friends, especially after German Navy U-boats sunk the passenger boat RMS *Lusitania* in May of 1915. More than a thousand innocent people died, including 123 Americans. People of the United States were outraged, but Germany said it would restrict U-boat attacks to military ships, so the Americans calmed down.

The British wanted the Americans to join the war. They believed that with American help, the Allies could end the war and stop the German Army. Nothing the British prime minister said could convince Woodrow Wilson of the need to help the Allies.

Early in 1917, Germany decided to break its promise of restricted submarine warfare and began sinking all types of vessels, including neutral ships and passenger boats. The American Congress was outraged, and cut off all diplomatic relations with Germany, but still did not declare war.

Because America was officially declared a neutral country, the Germans were allowed to use telegraph services at the U.S. embassies to send messages. What the Americans did not know was that the British Intelligence service had tapped the wires and was intercepting all of the messages that went out of the embassies. If the Americans found out about it, they would have become quite angry with the British for invading their privacy.

This caused quite a problem for the British when they intercepted a coded telegram from the Foreign Secretary of the German Empire, Arthur Zimmermann, to the German ambassador in Mexico. In the telegram, Zimmermann promised Mexico that it could have the states of New Mexico, Arizona, and Texas if it would go to war against the United States.

This was outrageous. Americans would be furious if they knew what Germany was proposing, but how could the British tell them without letting them know that they had been tapping the American telegraph lines? It was a problem.

The British came up with a plan. They had one of their agents in Mexico bribe the telegraph operator to give him a copy of the original telegram. This way, the British could say that their agent had "intercepted" the message in Mexico.

Woodrow Wilson received the message in February and released the full text to the press on February 28, 1917. As predicted, the American public was furious with Germany. By this time, Germany had also started sinking any and all ships, including American vessels. America declared war on Germany just a few weeks later. Just 19 months after America entered the war, Germany surrendered. Britain had been right. With the help of the Americans, the Allies won the war.

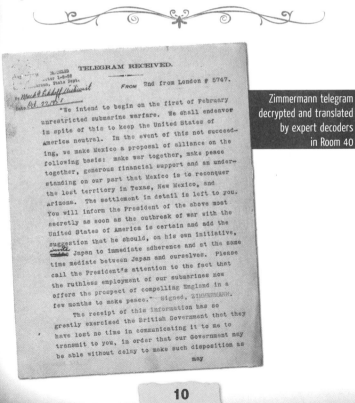

Zimmermann telegram decrypted and translated by expert decoders in Room 40

Most of the code breakers of World War I were not professionals when they began their jobs. They were people who were good at solving puzzles, math games, and word games. You can practice being a code breaker by playing the Decode It game.

Materials:

- ❏ Pencils
- ❏ Paper
- ❏ Partner

Play rock-paper-scissors to see which person will be the code breaker and who will be the code maker. After each round, you will switch jobs.

The code maker should choose four different numbers from 1–10. Write down the numbers. Don't let the code breaker see the numbers! (For example: the numbers might be 2, 6, 9, and 8.)

Next, the code breaker will try to guess the secret numbers in the correct order. The code breaker writes his guesses on a piece of paper and shows it to the code maker.

The code maker then uses a code to tell how close the guess is. The code maker can draw up to four small circles next to the guess. If the circle is filled in, it means one of the numbers is correct and in the correct position. If the circle is not filled in, it means a number is correct but in the wrong position. For example, if your friend guessed 2, 9, 5, 4, you'd draw one full circle and one empty circle. If he or she guessed 2, 9, 8, 4, you'd draw one full circle and two empty circles.

The code breaker then uses the information to make another guess. You will keep repeating this process until the code breaker gets the code right!

To score the game, the code maker gets one point for every guess the code breaker makes. Play five rounds and the code maker with the highest score is the winner.

Having trouble figuring out the Decode It game? Look at the photographs of this game in action at http://www. wikihow.com/Image:Play-Mastermind-With-a-Pencil-and-a-Piece-of-Paper-Step-7.jpg

Secret Society

Secret societies have been around for hundreds of years. Some, like the Black Hand, have bad intentions, but others exist to do good things. Sometimes people like to help others and remain anonymous, so they make a secret society or secret club. Other organizations are secret because they need to protect the identity of their members, like spy organizations. The secret societies usually have code names for their members and sometimes secret handshakes or code words.

You can make a secret society with your friends. First, you need to have a meeting and decide what secret activities you want to do. Maybe you want to help your neighborhood by picking up all of the trash or surprise your family by doing chores. That might be a big surprise! Think of something that would surprise people in a good way.

Then make up a secret name for your society. Do not tell the name to anyone except the people you invite to join. You should also create a secret password and a special handshake. Share this information with only your society members.

You can have lots of fun doing secret good works and watching as your family and neighbors wonder what is going on!

SPIES

THE SPY WITH THE WOODEN LEG

HOWARD BURNHAM

American Howard Burnham lost his leg in an accident when he was 14. Amputated 4 inches below the knee, he was fitted with a wooden leg and immediately learned how to ride horses, hunt, and track animals with his new appendage. He loved to read and had an amazing memory—so amazing that he could accurately recall almost anything he had read or heard.

Burnham made his living as a prospector and mine engineer and traveled the world looking for precious minerals and managing mines. He worked in South Africa, California, Germany, and Mexico, and taught in England. With his foreign language skills and knowledge of the world, he was the perfect candidate to become a spy. So much so that the French government recruited him to spy for them at the beginning of World War I.

On one assignment, he was asked to lead 28 soldiers into the desert of Algeria. Their mission was to negotiate peace between the Algerian rebels and the French government. Burnham and his team were ambushed by the rebels, and 20 of the men were killed. All of the rest, including Burnham, were taken prisoner. The only man to survive the ordeal was Burnham.

Even after such a terrifying experience, Burnham didn't give up his work for the Allies. His next assignment was to cross the Alps to Germany and learn about enemy troop positions. Burnham took on the mission even though he was suffering from a bad case of tuberculosis. He traveled through the mountains, secretly surveying the area for German Army installations. His cover was that he was traveling to health spas to help heal his tuberculosis. Burnham stored his survey tools in his wooden leg in case he was searched. He took no notes so that he would not be found with incriminating evidence and committed every detail to memory.

During his trip, his tuberculosis became much worse. When Burnham made it back to Switzerland, he was dying. The French government quickly moved Burnham to Cannes, France, and on his deathbed Burnham recited all of the surveys and information he had memorized. He assured the French that there was no need to send troops to the area, as there was no evidence of a Germany military buildup in the Alps. His spy work was invaluable to the French. It prevented them from wasting men and munitions and allowed them to concentrate their war efforts where there were real threats.

His dying words were: "Always have I wanted to help pay the debt my country has owed to France. Go back to the front and save the living. I am already dead."

A grateful French government honored Burnham and buried him in Cannes.

EDITH CAVELL
AND HER UNDERGROUND NETWORK

Edith Cavell, 1895

The wounded kept coming. Bloody and battered, Allied and German, it didn't matter what uniform they wore, Edith Cavell and her team of nurses treated them all. They ripped off shredded uniforms, bandaged gaping wounds, and treated each man with compassion and dignity. It was their duty. And Edith Cavell believed in doing her duty. Even when her duty meant she might face a firing squad.

As a young child in England, Edith accompanied her mother on visits to the poor and sick people in her father's parish. She helped pass out nourishing stews and bread and saw the difference it made to have warm, clean surroundings. As she grew older, Edith decided she wanted to study medicine and enrolled in nursing school. When most young women of that time period married and raised a family, Edith decided to pursue a career and worked as a head nurse and an instructor. She taught new nurses the importance of a clean and germ-free hospital. Her work was so successful that she was invited to help set up a hospital and training program in Belgium—she was working there when the Germans invaded.

Overnight, Edith and her nurses went from a Belgium hospital treating Allied soldiers to a Red Cross hospital charged with treating both friendly and enemy combatants. Red Cross rules clearly stated that Edith and her nurses were to treat each wounded man the same. They were to nurse them back to health and then turn them over to the army in charge. That was where Edith had a problem: She could not see the logic in nursing an Allied soldier back to health only to turn him over to the Germans, who would put the man in a prisoner of war camp. There had to be a way she could save the men and get them back to their units. Holland was right next to Belgium and the Germans had not yet invaded that country. Was there a way to smuggle the men out of the hospital and away from German prison camps?

Edith knew the risk she was taking. Helping the wounded Allied soldiers escape was considered treason by the occupying German Army. If she or anyone who helped her were caught, they would be killed. But Edith knew what she had to do. With the help of well-known architect Philippe Baucq, Edith was put in contact with the Prince and Princess de Croÿ. An underground network was established, with Edith smuggling the wounded soldiers out of the hospital and to a chateau owned by the Prince and Princess. From there, volunteer guides escorted the men across the border and into the freedom of Holland.

In less than a year's time, Edith and her underground network rescued some 200 Allied soldiers. It was a pace that could not be sustained. The Germans knew they were losing soldiers from the hospital, and Edith came under suspicion. The Germans ransacked the hospital and Edith's room looking for evidence, but Edith was meticulous. She had destroyed all papers and had sewn her personal diary into the cushion of her couch. The Germans left, but they were not satisfied.

A few days later, two members of the escape route team were arrested and information about both Edith and her friend Philippe Baucq was given to the Germans. Edith and Philipe were both arrested.

The American Red Cross
and World War I

The American Red Cross played an important role in WWI, with 18,000 nurses and 4,800 ambulance drivers providing first aid and medical care on the front lines. The organization worked hard to set up hospitals, distribute supplies and care packages, make artificial limbs, rehabilitate soldiers, and pioneer advances in medicine, such as psychiatric nursing hospitals for veterans. At home, the American Red Cross rallied Americans to donate funds to the service through its "Roll Call" campaign, which asked citizens to join the membership list for the organization by donating $1. The campaign was a huge success, helping raise $250 million for the organization.

Answer the
Red Cross
Christmas Roll Call

All you need is a heart
and a dollar

Edith was held in solitary confinement for nearly 10 weeks. She was interrogated by the Germans and freely admitted that she had smuggled Allied soldiers out of the country. She felt it was her duty to help in any way she could

and had no qualms in admitting what she had done. She knew she would be killed for her actions but said, "I have no fear nor shrinking; I have seen death so often that it is not strange or fearful to me."

Early on the morning of October 12, Edith Cavell, Philippe Baucq, and two other members of the escape route team were led outside and shot by a firing squad. They died immediately.

News of the gracious nurse's death spread quickly. People in England, France, and the United States were horrified that the Germans would kill a nurse who had helped the German soldiers. They could not believe they would be so brutal as to put her in front of a firing squad. The Germans could not understand the outrage of the Allied people. The German Minister of Foreign Affairs issued the statement, "It was a pity that Miss Cavell had to be executed, but it was necessary. She was judged justly. We hope it will not be necessary to have any more executions."

This statement just made the Allied people more angry and throughout the rest of the war people were told to "remember Nurse Cavell." Historians believe that the sinking of the Lusitania and the death of Edith Cavell were two important events that brought the United States into The Great War.

ACE OF SPIES

SIDNEY REILLY

He had passports with 11 different names. He was a master of disguise and could speak at least six languages. He had numerous girlfriends and married several of them. He was the model for author Ian Fleming's fictional spy, James Bond. He was Sidney Reilly.

Born in Russia in 1874, he was named Georgi Rosenblum. Not much is known of his early life (in fact, many theories abound about his childhood and background). He liked to tell people that he left home at 19 and spent time as a train engineer in India, a bouncer in Brazil, and worked as a spy for the Japanese government. His stories may be true, or they could be the lies of a very sneaky spy.

What is known and documented is that Sidney Reilly was employed as a spy for the British Secret Intelligence Service

MI6 in 1909. His assignment was to go to Germany and get information about the build-up of the German war machine. His cover was to become a shipyard worker named Karl Khan. He was supposed to find a way to get copies of ship plans. Reilly soon discovered that the plant was heavily guarded, so he volunteered to work the night shift. After a few nights working and scouting out the plant, Reilly killed one guard and overpowered another and stole the plans. He hopped a train, then a boat, staying hidden from German agents and eventually making it back to England with the plans.

Because he was successful in getting the plans from Germany, he was sent on a new mission to Russia to learn what was happing in that country. Reilly set himself up as an arms distributor complete with a real company. His company was awarded the contracts to rebuild the Russian fleet, with the designs based on the German fleet. When Reilly's company got the plans, he sent photocopies back to England. Reilly also arranged to keep all of the profits from his newly formed company. If there was a way to profit from spying, Reilly found it.

When war broke out, Reilly was living in luxury in New York City. He worked for a while for the Russian government, buying the Russian Army guns and munitions from the United States and Japan. Again, the work was very profitable, and it didn't seem to matter to Reilly which country he worked for as long as he was well paid.

Toward the end of the war, Britain called on Reilly for help. This time, they wanted him to help keep Russia in the war fighting against Germany. In 1918, the Russians had signed a peace treaty with Germany, but Britain wanted them to keep fighting the Germans. Reilly's job was to find a way to get Russia back in the war. Reilly's idea was to overthrow the new Russian government, but it didn't go too well and Reilly barely escaped Russia without being killed.

But Britain had one more job for Reilly. They needed information about the German army. Reilly spoke fluent

German, so he joined the army and sent messages back to England via carrier pigeon.

Reilly also claimed to have impersonated German officers to get into high-level meetings and spy on their war plans. No one knows if this was really true, because there is no written evidence, but Reilly did give enough information to the British to be awarded the Military Cross for "gallantry during active operations against the enemy."

After the war, Reilly continued his espionage work within Russia and tried to help overthrow the new government. He made a lot of enemies in the Russian government and in 1925, he was captured and shot by a firing squad.

The legend of Sidney Reilly has lived on in fiction books, movies, and even televisions shows. It is still hard to know which stories about Reilly were true and which ones were part of his vivid imagination, but everyone agrees that Sidney Reilly was definitely the Ace of Spies.

The Real James Bond?

Sidney Reilly wasn't just the Ace of Spies, he was partly the real-life inspiration for Ian Fleming's character, James Bond. Fleming was friends with Sir Robert Lockhart, who told him about Reilly's famous exploits. This, in combination with Fleming's own training and experience with the British Intelligence, is thought to have influenced many of his famous stories of super-spy James Bond.

MATA HARI

Mata Hari, 1905

At dawn on October 15, 1917, Mata Hari was awakened in her prison cell by two nuns and told that her time had come. She quickly wrote two letters and left them for her lawyer, then put on her silk stockings, high heels, and fur-lined cloak and made her way silently to the firing range.

Twelve French soldiers were armed and ready. Mata Hari stood in front of them sober and silent. She was offered a blindfold but refused. The signal was given and the 12 soldiers took aim and fired. The famous dancer Mata Hari was dead, killed as an enemy spy.

As a dancer, Mata Hari loved to make people think her life was exotic and mysterious. She claimed to be a Javanese princess who had been raised in a temple in India, and performed her native dances for thousands of people during the early 1900s. In reality, she was Margaretha "Margreet" Zelle MacLeod, the daughter of a hat maker from the Netherlands.

When she was a child, Margreet had been doted on by her father. He ran a very successful hat making company at a time when custom required all men to wear hats. One of her toys as a child was a miniature carriage that was pulled by two goats. She grew up in a wealthy home until she was a teenager. Then, a series of tragedies struck the family. Her father went bankrupt and her mother died. Margreet was sent to live with relatives, but felt alone and unloved so she answered an advertisement in the newspaper and married a man 20 years older. He was an officer in the military and they moved to Indonesia, where Margreet studied the culture, customs, and dances.

Unfortunately for Margreet, it was a very unhappy marriage because the man was abusive. After a few years, she left her husband and returned to Europe. Alone and penniless, she decided to use her dance skills to earn money, becoming an instant sensation on the Paris stage with her glamorous costumes and unusual dancing.

Many men and women of the time thought her dancing was scandalous, because she wore a flesh-colored body stocking and took off layers of scarves until the audience could see much of her body. This was at a time when most women were embarrassed to show their ankles.

As a famous dancer, she also had many male admirers, including several high-ranking German officials. Some of these were the chief of the Berlin police; Alfred Kiepert, a lieutenant in the German Army; and Karl Kroemer, the German consul in Amsterdam.

Because of her close connections with the Germans, Mata Hari was asked by one French official to pass on any information she learned. Mata Hari agreed to help, but apparently the information she gave the French was deemed worthless. The French decided she must be spying for the Germans.

Mata Hari was detained and questioned. She admitted that she had told German officials useless information too, but denied that she was a spy. She told them that she was spying for the French, but it had never been made official and nobody believed her. Mata Hari was sent to trial and convicted of spying.

Was she really a spy or was she just trying to keep all of her admirers happy by telling them things they wanted to hear? Historical records give no hard evidence either way, but when she was killed it made news worldwide. The famous Mata Hari had been convicted of espionage and killed. Books and movies have been made about her life, but the truth died with Mata Hari at dawn on October 15, 1917.

Mata Hari, 1910

LA DAME BLANCHE

Henry Landau had a tough assignment. He was to set up and coordinate a spy network to send information out of Belgium to France. It was an area full of small farming communities with small stores and quiet laborers. Where was he going to find people who could be spies that could outwit the German Army?

He found them in the everyday people of Belgium. The shopkeepers and farmers and their wives and children became train watchers, going about their daily business, but always watching the trains that rolled through Belgium.

Landau's network of everyday spies became known as La Dame Blanche. It was named after a legend that the appearance of the White Lady would be a sign that the German Kaiser would fall from power.

The members of La Dame Blanche did not communicate with each other. It was safer if they did not know who else was in the spy ring. They communicated with Landau through drop boxes. When they had information about German troops being shipped on trains, they coded a note and left it at a drop box. The boxes were inside shops, bars, or post offices. Certain spies were assigned to collect the messages and get across the border of Belgium to the Netherlands, where Landau and his colleagues would coordinate all of the information.

Members of La Dame Blanche knew their information was vital to the war effort and whole families worked at collecting information. Families who lived near the rail lines kept watch 24 hours a day. Children would watch while parents were working, and someone was assigned the task of night watch to see what the Germans were shipping under cover of darkness.

Henry Landau and the La Dame Blanche team were quite successful—it is estimated that 70% of all the valuable intelligence that came out of Belgium was delivered by the White Lady spies.

ARCHAEOLOGIST SPY SYLVANUS MORLEY

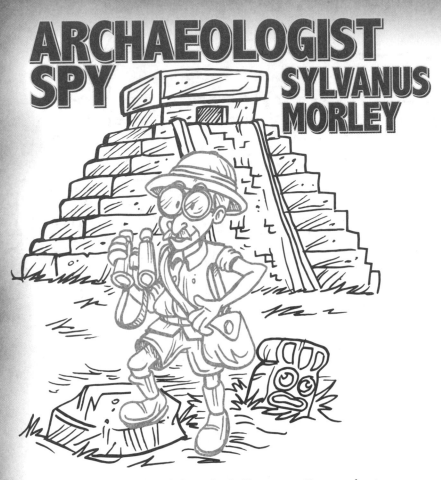

Sylvanus Morley did not look like a spy. He was short, skinny, wore glasses, and studied archaeology. He looked more like a rumpled college professor than an international spy, but Slyvanus Morley was the best American spy in World War I.

After America learned about Germany's plot for Mexico to attack the United States, the military decided it needed spies in Central America. The American Navy was especially worried that Germans would put submarine bases along the coast of Central America and sink U.S. ships. They needed a spy who could speak Spanish and travel without looking suspicious. Sylvanus Morley was just the man for the job.

As an archaeologist, Morley had already traveled through many areas of Central America and he knew how dangerous it was. Once when Morley and his team were exploring the Mayan ruins, they were attacked by Guatemalan soldiers. Two of Morley's team were shot and killed. Morley only escaped being killed because he had dropped his glasses. He stopped his horse and got off to pick up his glasses while the rest of the group rode on ahead. Morley had just retrieved his glasses when he heard shots ring out. He yelled for everyone to turn around but it was too late. Morley was deeply impacted by the loss of his team members, but it didn't stop him from volunteering himself as a spy for the American Office of Naval Intelligence (ONI).

In March of 1917, the ONI gratefully accepted Morley's offer, and in less than a month, he had been issued communication codes and secret names for his contacts. He was to send his letters to Taro Yamamoto and Adolph Schwartz. The Japanese and German names were to try to fool counterspies.

Morley recruited his own partner, John Held, who was a noted artist and cartoonist. Their cover would be as an archaeologist and mapmaker searching for ancient ruins. It was true. They did survey for Mayan ruins, but they also looked for German spies, weapons, and possible military build-up.

For the next 14 months, Morley and Held traveled through rugged mountains and soggy rainforests. They rode on stubborn mules, and when the trails were too treacherous for the mules, they walked. They suffered from bug bites and stings and a terrible infestation of fleas. At one point Morley was so miserable from all of the bites that he took a bath in whiskey. In his diary, he reported that while it stung horribly, the whiskey did help.

Wherever they went, Morley took notes and Held drew pictures. When they reached any place with a mail train, they sent information back to Yamamoto and Schwartz. During their travels, they had many narrow escapes. They were mis-

taken for Guatemalan rebels, accused of being German spies, and suspected of being American spies, but did not get caught.

Held became so sick with dysentery (diarrhea and fever) that he had to be hospitalized. Morley continued his work without Held until he became sick with malaria. When they were both well, they teamed up and went back out into the jungle.

After an extensive search, Morley concluded that there were no German submarine bases in Central America. This news was extremely important, because it freed up the American military to concentrate its efforts on the European arena instead of having to waste resources to guard the southern borders of the United States.

At the end of the war, Morley kept working in Central America, but he focused on his archaeology studies. He became a world expert on the Mayan culture and is credited with the discovery of Uaxactun. He also oversaw most of the excavations of the ancient Mayan site, Chichen Itza. Morley became well known as a Mayan scholar and led many archaeological digs and tours. He was still leading tours just a few months before his death in 1948 at the age of 65.

Morley never talked about his days as a spy and was never recognized by the Navy until decades after his death.

BRAVE BELGIAN SPY

MARTHE CNOCKAERT

All that was left of Marthe Cnockaert's childhood home was a pile of rubble and burnt timbers. The German army had marched through West Flanders, Belgium, in August of 1914, burning and destroying the cities they captured. Marthe's home was one of those that were demolished. In the confusion of the invasion, 22-year-old Marthe had been separated from her family. Now she was alone in a town full of German military with the war raging all around.

Marthe needed a way to earn a living and stay alive, so she volunteered her services to the local hospital that was now being run by the Germans. Her training as a nurse made her quite valuable in the eyes of the Germans. She was assigned work as a nurse and was soon caring for the soldiers of the army that had devastated her home.

Marthe truly cared about the individual soldiers. She worked hard to help them heal and made them as comfortable as possible. She was awarded the German Iron Cross for all of her hard work on her patients' behalf, but she hated the German invasion of her homeland and was anxious to do something to help the resistance.

In 1915, Marthe was transferred to the German Military hospital in Roulers, Belgium, where she was reunited with her family. Her parents were running a restaurant and when Marthe was not working at the hospital she spent her time waitressing. Hard-working Marthe caught the attention of neighbor Lucelle Deldonck. Lucelle was working undercover as a British intelligence agent and she thought Marthe would make an excellent spy.

Marthe agreed and was immediately put to work. She was given the code name Laura and signed all of her messages with a simple L. For 2 years, Marthe joked and flirted with the German officers who visited the hospital and ate at the restaurant, while listening for information on troop movements and clues as to where the Germans were planning to strike next.

She worked with two other female Belgian spies to get her messages to the British. "Canteen Ma" was the code name for an elderly lady who was a vegetable seller. None of the Germans suspected that an old woman would be spying for the British, and Marthe often passed her information through "Canteen Ma."

Her other contact was a letterbox agent simply known as "Number 63." This agent made sure that Marthe's written communication made it through the enemy lines and into the

Allied hands. For 2 years, Marthe and her sister spies gave the British important information about German troop movements and plans inside Belgium.

During that time, Marthe's family was forced to provide housing to a German officer, and he was determined to recruit Marthe to be a spy for the Germans. At first she tried to play along and gave him bits of useless information, but the German spy became more and more insistent that Marthe give him information. He began to threaten her and spy on her movements. Marthe reported her problems to her fellow spies and just a few weeks later the German lodger suddenly died.

Not long after that, Marthe discovered an unused sewer system that ran directly under the German ammunition depot. Armed with explosives, Marthe crawled through the

The German Spies

Germany used spies to help gather information, too, of course. Often, they worked to follow suspected spies from other countries, like **Madeleine Zabriskie Doty**, an American activist who decided to enter Germany to see what the conditions were like for the people living there during wartime. Doty was constantly being watched—and she knew it. As she wrote, "**The funny thing about German spies** is that they dress for the part. They are as unmistakable as Sherlock Holmes. They nearly always wear gray clothes, a soft gray hat, are pale-faced, shifty-eyed, smooth-shaven, or have only a slight moustache, and carry canes."

filthy tight tunnels and carefully laid down bombs that could destroy the ammo. She made it out and, with the help of another spy, blew up the German's ammunition.

The Germans immediately launched an investigation— unfortunately they found a clue that led them to Marthe. She had lost her gold watch engraved with her name. The Germans arrested Marthe, and in November of 1916, she was sentenced to death for being a spy.

Thrown into a German prison, Marthe was tortured and beaten by the German soldiers in the hope that she would give them information about the other spies. Marthe refused to talk. She went on a hunger strike saying she would rather starve to death than give up the names of her fellow spies.

Marthe became ill and weak, and the Germans sent a Belgian woman in to nurse Marthe. But even in her weakened condition, Marthe knew it was a trap. She refused to talk to the woman and eventually she was removed from the cell.

Fraulein Doktor

She was wanted by the British MI6; a mysterious woman only known as Fraulein Doktor. She was credited with training the most successful German spies. She taught them how to use different names and identities and how to trick people into giving out secret information. German spies who were captured never uttered her real name and the British never captured her. Now 100 years after the start of the war, no one knows for sure who the master spy teacher was, but several movies have been made about her adventures.

The woman was indeed a spy for the Germans, but she never got any information from Marthe.

The German doctors at the hospital had great admiration for Marthe and the work she had done to save the lives of many German soldiers. They pleaded with the German officers and testified on her behalf, telling the officers that it would be horribly wrong to kill a woman who had been awarded the Iron Cross for her service to the German soldiers. Finally, it was agreed that Marthe would not be executed, but she remained in prison until the end of the war in 1918.

After the war, Marthe wrote a book about her adventures as a spy. She also wrote several spy novels and a movie was even made about her life. Marthe died in 1966 at the age of 73.

Marthe Cnockaert, 1914

SPY TRAINING
Camouflage Yourself

The secret to being a great spy is to be able hide in the middle of a crowd. You need to blend in or camouflage yourself. That means you have to look right for each place you are planning to be a spy. Going to spy on someone at a football game? Make sure you look like one of the crowd. Wear a football jersey for the right team and a cap with the same logo. If you are going to be spying at a fancy party, you don't want to show up in grungy clothes. You need to look the part.

The secret to disguising yourself is to make changes that will help you fit in with the crowd around you. You don't want to stand out; you need to blend in. Think about where you will be doing your spying. Will you be at a library? Make sure you can hide behind a stack of books and reading glasses. If you are spying at the mall, you need to look like one of the other shoppers. Carry a shopping bag and wear casual clothes.

Think about the situations where you will be spying and dress appropriately. You don't need a fake moustache and nose (that will only make you stand out!). You can practice by trying out your spy skills in the following situations:

1. *Spying at home:* Pretend to be watching television, but instead listen to what people are saying around you.

2. *Spying at school or the library:* Put your nose in a book but keep your eyes open. Take note of who goes where and what they are doing.

3. *Spying at the park:* Take your dog for a walk. You can follow people and listen to their conversations while you pretend to let your dog wander around the park. Don't have a dog? Ask a friend to help you by pretending to play catch or Frisbee.

With a little practice, you can learn to be a successful spy that blends into a crowd and learns all of the best secrets.

SPY TRAINING
Hidden in Plain Sight

Howard Burnham hid his spy tools in his wooden leg. Nobody thought to look there. His leg was in plain sight, but no one checked it for spy equipment. You can be like master spy Howard Burnham and hide your secret papers and treasures in plain sight by making a fake rock.

Materials:

- ❑ Help from an adult
- ❑ Old newspapers or magazines
- ❑ Modpodge or a mixture of 2/3 white glue and 1/3 water
- ❑ A small inflated balloon
- ❑ Gray or brown paint
- ❑ Paintbrush

First, inflate the balloon to the size of a child's fist. This will be the hollow part of the "rock," where you will be able to hide treasures. Tear the newspaper or magazine into strips. Dip the strips into the glue mixture and layer it over the balloon. Leave the bottom uncovered. Let the first layer dry. Keep adding layers. Make it look rough like the surface of a rock.

When you have the shape you want, you can pop the balloon. It should leave a hollow space where you can hide treasures. Then paint your hiding space so that it looks like a rock. Disguise it in your flowerbed or driveway. You are ready to hide your secrets in plain sight, just like Howard Burnham.

SPECIAL MISSIONS

RAZZLE DAZZLE

The Allied Navy had a serious problem. Its ships were being sunk at an alarming rate. German U-boats (submarines) sank five British cruisers in the first 10 weeks of war. On September 22, 1915, the German torpedoes sank three ships in one hour. The Fleet Admiral knew he needed help, so what did he do? He called in an artist, of course.

Artist and British naval officer Norman Wilkinson came up with a unique solution to the problem. He decided to paint naval ships in purple and yellow stripes and other brightly colored geometric patterns. It was not a form of camouflage; it was a way to confuse the enemy and mislead them as to the correct position of the ship.

In World War I, there were no radars, lasers, or heat sensors. Sinking a battleship was a time-consuming and tedious

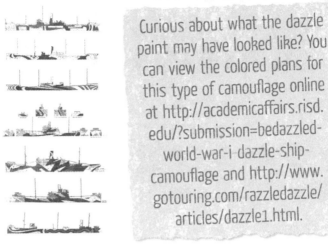

Curious about what the dazzle paint may have looked like? You can view the colored plans for this type of camouflage online at http://academicaffairs.risd.edu/?submission=bedazzled-world-war-i-dazzle-ship-camouflage and http://www.gotouring.com/razzledazzle/articles/dazzle1.html.

process that involved locating the target and calculating the ship's speed and heading. Once that was calculated, the torpedo was launched, but it was not aimed directly at the ship. Instead it was aimed to where the navy officer *thought* the ship was going to be by the time the torpedo traveled through the ocean. Dazzle camouflage made it difficult for the enemy to determine the type of ship, the speed, or the heading. This made it much more challenging to send the torpedo in the right direction at the right time. It didn't hide the ships, but it made them much harder to hit.

Dazzle paint made it difficult for the enemy to see what kind of ship was near them. The brightly colored stripes and lines disrupted the rangefinders. Observers couldn't tell whether the stern or bow of the ship was in view. They couldn't tell if the ship were coming at them or sailing away. It became much more difficult for the U-boats to sink the battleships.

Photographs of World War I are all in black and white, so it is a little hard to imagine the purple, red, and yellow ships. The colored plans give an idea of what the actual dazzle paint ships looked like.

A Few Examples of
RAZZLE DAZZLE DESIGNS

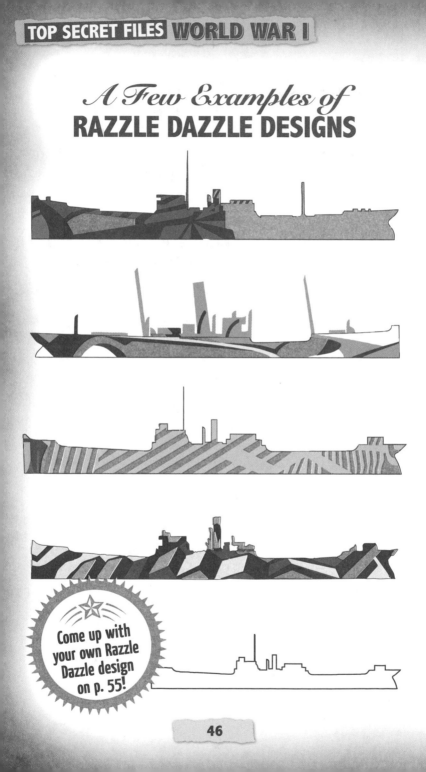

Come up with your own Razzle Dazzle design on p. 55!

Q-SHIPS

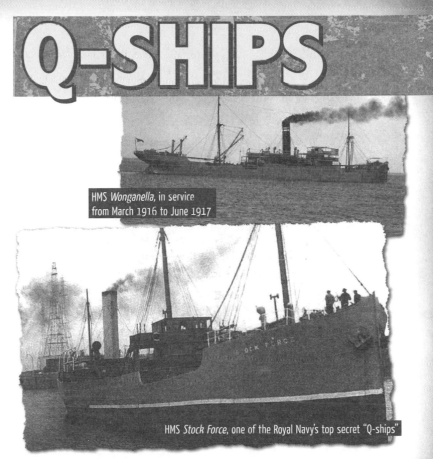

HMS *Wonganella*, in service from March 1916 to June 1917

HMS *Stock Force*, one of the Royal Navy's top secret "Q-ships"

The German U-boats (submarines) were a nightmare for the Allies. Big, silent, and fast running, they sank Allied ships faster than the Allied countries could build them. The Allies had only developed submarines that ran underwater for short distances and could be used for coastal patrols. They did not have any underwater craft that was a match for the U-boat.

On September 22, 1914, it took only one German U-boat to sink three British Royal Navy cruisers. At this rate, the Allied Navy would be decimated. Something had to be done, so the Allies came up with a plan.

The rules of warfare in 1914 were the same they had been for almost 50 years. The 1856 Declaration of Paris stated that

> " . . . passenger ships may not be sunk,
> crews of merchant ships must be placed
> in safety before their ships may be sunk
> (life boats are not considered a place of
> safety unless close to land); and only
> warships and merchant ships that are
> a threat to the attacker may be sunk
> without warning. "

This meant that a submarine was supposed to hail a ship before it attacked and let the crew and passengers escape.

The Allies decided to use this to their advantage. They took old fishing boats and flat freighter ships and made a fake deck on the ships. Then they hid guns on the ship. The code name for these fake boats was "Q-ship."

When the German U-boat would hail the Q-ship and give warning of an attack, the Q-ship crew would drop a boat in the water and a few men would row away. This made it look like the crew was escaping the boat. Then the U-boat would move in closer to launch the torpedo. As soon as the U-boat moved, the Q-ship dropped the fake deck and raised the guns. Then they fired on the U-boat. The surprise attack would drive the U-boat back and protect real Navy vessels.

It was an incredibly dangerous job. The crews on the Q-ships were basically decoys waiting to be fired on by submarines. In the beginning, the Q-ships were very successful and quickly sank 11 German U-boats. But later in the war, Germany declared "unrestricted warfare," which meant that they no longer gave a warning before attacking. Then the Q-ships were less effective in destroying the U-boats, but they still acted as decoys, protecting the real Navy vessels from attack. The Q-ships were successful enough in World War I that the Allies used them again in World War II.

SPY TREES IN NO MAN'S LAND

A canvas and steel tree observation post near Souchez, France, May 1918

No man's land. Pockmarked with bomb holes and empty of plant life, a few stumps of trees were all that stood in the strip of land between the Allies' front line and the German trenches. Soldiers who dared to poke their head up above the trench line were asking to be shot. If a soldier went down in no man's land, he could be left for dead. Friends who tried to rescue the wounded were destined to be blasted with gunfire. Neither side could cross and neither side would back down. It was a stalemate. A tie.

Until the day British engineers had the bright idea of turning the raggedy tree stumps into spy lookouts. It was the perfect plan, but it took a lot of work. An engineer at the front line selected a tree stump that was wide enough to hold a fully grown man. He crawled through the front lines to photograph, sketch, and measure the tree in detail. The information was then sent back to a workshop where artists built an artificial tree to match the stump in no man's land. The inside of the fake tree was made from hollow steel cylinders with scaffolding inside so a man could climb up and down. Special holes were made so the soldier could spy with binoculars or shoot with a sniper rifle.

Christmas Truce of 1914

German soldiers of the 134th Saxon Regiment photographed with men of the Royal Warwickshire Regiment in no man's land on the Western Front, December 26, 1914

No one dared to venture into no man's land. Except on Christmas Day, 1914, where the soldiers from the German and British trenches came together to exchange food and souvenirs and to mingle. Carols were sung and joint burial ceremonies performed. There's even a documented case of a joint soccer game! The unofficial ceasefire is well known as a symbolic moment of peace, goodwill, and humanity during the war.

When the fake tree was finished, it was sent back to no man's land, where the British waited for the cover of darkness. When night came, the soldiers snuck into no man's land with picks and shovels. They worked quietly to tear down the real tree stump and replace it with the fake tree. It all had to be done in one night, or they would be caught and the Germans would discover their secret.

Once the soldiers had dug out the tree, they had to haul the wood back to their trench. The fake tree was then put together on the exact same spot. In the morning, German lookouts would see the same tree that was there the night before. They would not suspect that the new tree housed a soldier ready to spy on their camp or a sniper ready to shoot.

The fake trees were quite successful. No man's land was a flat area and even the slight elevation of the fake trees gave spies and snipers the advantage. Fake trees became a very popular way of spying, and by the end of the war, there were about 45 fake trees in use. Today the only remaining spy tree is on display at the Imperial War Museum in London.

A *camouflage tree* was an observation post of hollow metal construction shaped to look like a dead tree. The camouflage tree was designed and constructed under the supervision of the portrait painter Solomon J. Solomon and was erected on the bank of the Yser canal on March 1916. Lt. Col. Solomon and Mr. Walter Russell, who assisted him at the Royal Engineers Camouflage Works, are seen to the right of the picture.

© IWM (Art.IWM ART 6476)

Before war broke out, the French people were in love with the new invention of the airplane. Paris was the site for heart-pounding air races and amazing displays of the newest type of plane. But war taught the French that the airplane could be used to cause death and destruction. German planes flew over the country and dropped bombs on businesses and homes. Pilots sprayed the ground with machine gun bullets and the French people were afraid.

What if Germany decided to send many planes filled with bombs and drop them on the beautiful city of Paris? Something had to be done. But how could they save Paris and its residents? No one had invented defense missiles yet. Radar had not been invented yet to tell the people that the planes were coming. What could they possibly do to save Paris?

The French air defense group (Défense contre avions) had an idea. What if they could fool the German pilots into bombing the wrong Paris? If they could build a place that looked like Paris from the air, maybe they could make the pilots drop the bombs in the wrong place and save the real city. French officials thought the idea might just work.

Dropping bombs in WWI was not a scientific process guided by laser and radar. To drop a bomb, the crew of the airplane would hold bombs by the fins and then drop them on any target they could see. The pilot had to fly low enough for the crew to see the target, but high enough that the plane would not be blown up in the explosion. The planes carried a limited amount of fuel, so they had to make their bombing runs very short. It would be possible to fool the German aircrews if they built a good replica of Paris.

In 1918, planners selected a site 15 miles from away from the heart of Paris by the small town of Maisons-Laffitte. There they began building a fake city that would look like Paris from the air. Builders laid out roads that looked like the streets of Paris. They constructed wooden replicas of homes, schools, and factories. During WWI, factories often had glass roofs to let in enough light for the workers. Painters used translucent paint to look like the dirty glass roofs of Parisian factories.

A replica of the train station was built and fake railroad tracks were laid down. Electrical engineer Fernand Jacopozzi was hired to create lighting that would make the fake Paris look real. He used white, red, and yellow lamps to give the illusion of machines working at night and lit up the fake train stations and roads.

But the fake Paris never got the chance to be tested. The war ended in November of 1918. Parisians were relieved. The builders tore down the fake buildings and hid the plans. They wanted to keep the secret of the fake city just in case they might need to fool another army another time. No one talked about the fake city, and the French began to love the airplane again and started to put on international air shows that are still held each year in Paris.

Light Up the Night

After the war ended, electrical engineer Fernand Jacopozzi was hired to illuminate the Eiffel Tower. His light display was so successful that he earned the nickname "The Magician of Light."

Dazzle Effect

SPY TRAINING

The dazzle effect that was used by the artists in World War I is being studied today by computer programmers and other techies looking for ways to fool facial recognition software. It is called CV Dazzle and uses techniques similar to the dazzle ships to confuse modern computer optics.

You can see examples of the facial dazzle below and at http://cvdazzle.com/.

You can create your own dazzle camouflage on the next page with markers or crayons. Be sure to use bold lines and geometric shapes.

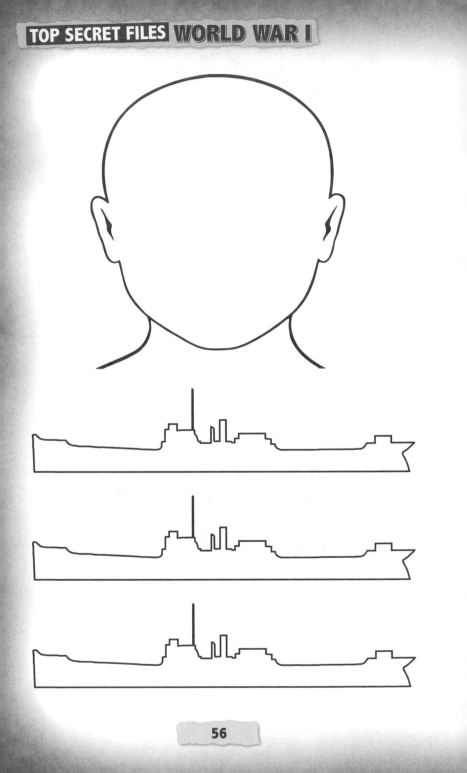

Build a Decoy

The Q-ships were designed to be decoys to fool the U-boats into attacking them. A decoy can be anything that can lure someone into a trap or fool him into thinking it is something it is not. You can build a candy jar decoy that will fool your friends or siblings. Just leave it out in plain sight and see who tries to eat some of your candy!

Materials:

❑ A clear glass or plastic jar

❑ White school glue

❑ Some hard candy such as peppermints or jawbreakers

Put the candy in your jar. Then pour the white glue over the candy. You will need to let it dry for at least 24 hours so that it looks clear.

When your decoy jar of candy is dry, set it out in your room and hide yourself somewhere that you can spy on people who visit your room. Watch and see how many people try to take a piece of candy from your decoy jar.

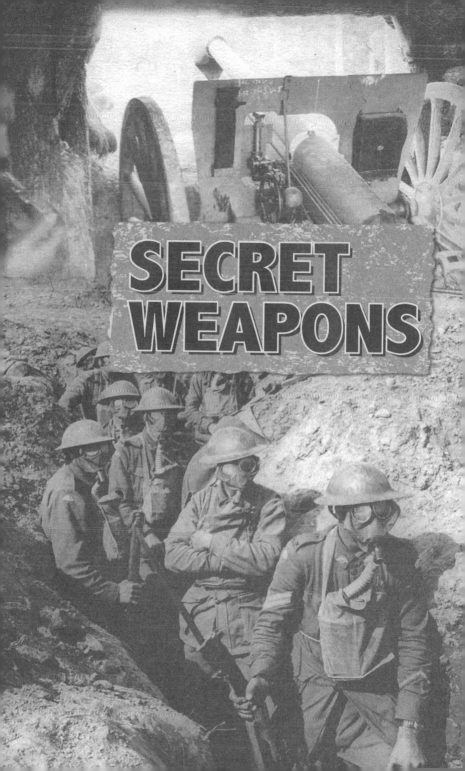

SECRET WEAPONS

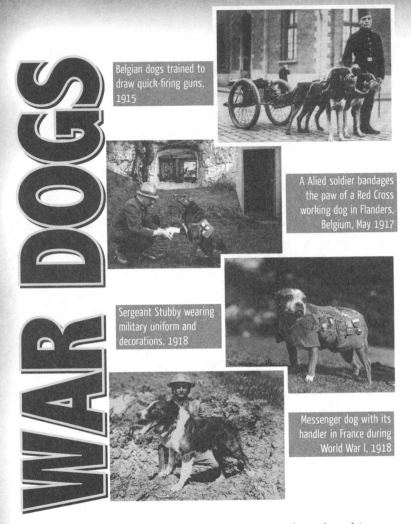

WAR DOGS

Belgian dogs trained to draw quick-firing guns, 1915

A Alied soldier bandages the paw of a Red Cross working dog in Flanders, Belgium, May 1917

Sergeant Stubby wearing military uniform and decorations, 1918

Messenger dog with its handler in France during World War I, 1918

Stubby heard a strange noise near the trenches where his American soldiers were camped. He crept out of the trench and went to investigate. What he found was a German spy sketching a map of the Allied trenches. Stubby knew what he had to do. He gave a deep growl and attacked the spy, biting at his heels and tearing at his clothes.

By the time Stubby's friends heard the commotion, Stubby had knocked the spy to the ground and bit him on the seat of his pants. Because of this and his many other acts of heroism, Sergeant Stubby became the most decorated dog in all of World War I.

Stubby may have been one of the most famous dogs who served in the war, but he was not the only dog on the battlefield. It is estimated that there were more than 20,000 dogs serving in the military on both sides of WWI. Dogs were trained to act as scouts and sentry guards, to help medics on the battlefield, and to relay messages to the front.

Sentry dogs were trained to stand guard and never to bark if they heard a stranger approach. Instead, the sentry dog would prick up its ears and point to the direction it heard the intruder so the soldier would know to be on guard.

Messenger dogs had the most dangerous job. They were trained to take messages to and from headquarters and the front lines. Dogs were used when it was too dangerous to send a human messenger. The dogs were lower to the ground and ran much faster than humans. They were often able to get messages through when human soldiers could not.

Medic dogs were trained to search on the battlefield for wounded soldiers. They carried medical kits that they took out to the soldiers who were wounded and stranded in no man's land. They were also used to sniff out survivors in bombed-out buildings.

Sergeant Stubby was never formally trained, but instinctively acted as a medic dog. He would search and find wounded soldiers on the battlefield and wait with them until help arrived. Stubby suffered from being attacked with poisonous gas. After he recovered he was very sensitive to the gas and would bark and warn the soldiers to get their gas masks on. He saved many soldiers from death by poison gas.

Stubby was wounded in a grenade attack but was rushed to the field hospital and saved. While he was recovering, he spent time visiting with the wounded soldiers and helped raise their morale.

At the end of the war, Stubby went home with the young soldier who had smuggled him across the ocean from America.

Stubby marched in and led many parades and met Presidents Woodrow Wilson, Calvin Coolidge, and Warren G. Harding.

In 1921, Stubby's master, Robert Conroy, began attending Georgetown law school, so of course, Stubby went to school, too. He became the Georgetown Hoyas' team mascot. He died at the ripe old age of 70 dog years.

War Horses & Elephant Farmers

Cars and trucks were new inventions in World War I, so horses were still used to carry supplies, pull wagons, and move artillery. It is estimated that the British army had 870,000 horses working in the war. Dead horses were melted down for fat, which was later used for making explosives.

Because horses throughout Britain were commandeered for use by the Army, many farmers were left without any horses to pull their plows. A few lucky farmers were able to make use of circus elephants to help with the farm chores. During the war, everyone had to do their part, including the circus animals.

U-BOATS
A SOPHISTICATED SUBMARINE

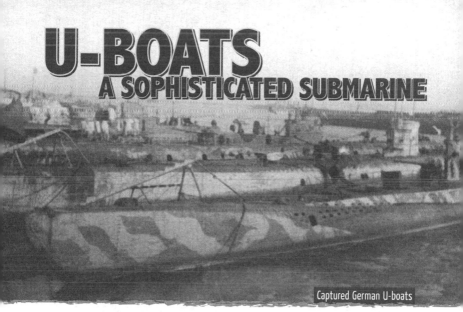

Captured German U-boats

Germany built its first submarine in 1851. It sank on its initial voyage, but the Germans kept working with submarines, experimenting and improving them. By the start of WWI, Germany had 29 Unterseeboots, nicknamed U-boats by the British.

The German U-boat was far more sophisticated than any submarine of any other country. A typical German U-boat was 214 feet long, carried 35 men, had 12 torpedoes, and could travel underwater for 2 hours at a time. It was a fighting machine.

By contrast, British admirals had not spent time or resources developing submarines. They considered fighting with submarines to be "under-handed, unfair, and dashed un-English." They had only developed "K"-class submarines that earned the nickname Kalamity Class. The K-class submarines had so many accidents that a third of them sank without being hit by enemy fire.

Because the British and French had not developed their own fighting class of submarine, they were totally unprepared for the threat of the U-boats. Within the first 10 weeks of the war, the German U-boats sank five British cruisers.

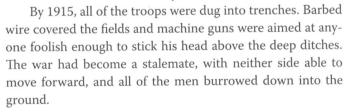

LITTLE WILLIE

By 1915, all of the troops were dug into trenches. Barbed wire covered the fields and machine guns were aimed at anyone foolish enough to stick his head above the deep ditches. The war had become a stalemate, with neither side able to move forward, and all of the men burrowed down into the ground.

There had to be a way to move the troops out of the trenches and end the war. Britain began researching and came up with a vehicle that could blow through the barbed wire and roll over the trenches. They named the new vehicle Little Willie.

It was the first land tank ever invented, and it looked like a metal box on caterpillar tracks. Little Willy was 9 feet tall and weighed 16.5 tons and had a gun turret on the top. Inside was a simple bench for the driver and crew and it could hold six men. It rolled along at the amazingly fast rate of 2 miles per hour. Slower than a soldier on foot. But Willie was shielded with metal and could move through gunfire. Lord Admiral Winston Churchill was impressed with Willie's potential and ordered further tanks to be developed.

The next tank was called Big Willie, or Mother. The new tank was 10 feet tall and weighed 28 tons. The big machine was able to roll over trenches that were 9 feet wide and plow over barbed wire like it was string.

There were problems with Mother. Inside the tank, temperatures could rise to more than 100 degrees Fahrenheit and the power plant was sometimes unreliable. But it was the best hope for ending the trench warfare and moving the Germans back.

Both the French and British kept building and improving their tank forces. By the end of the war, Britain had produced more than 2,600 and the French had built more than 3,800. The Germans had built only 20.

The tanks did the job they were designed to do and stopped the trench warfare. Hiding in a deep trench became useless when a giant tank could roll right over you. The tanks moved the soldiers back out of the trenches and helped end the war.

On September 15, 1916, the Allies sent 32 tanks rolling into the fight in Somme, France. The tanks led the way with the infantry following behind. Some of the tanks got mired down in the deep mud and some suffered breakdowns, but 21 of the tanks plowed through the barbed wire defenses and the Germans retreated rather than face the metal giants. The tanks were deemed a success.

Inside
the Tank

Splatter mask worn by
tank crews in WWI

Being a soldier inside a tank was hard duty. The
temperatures could rise to 122 degrees F. There was
no air filtration system, so the soldiers were breathing
carbon monoxide. Sometime entire crews passed out.
Tank crews also had to wear helmets, goggles, and
chain mail masks to protect them from rivets and flying
pieces of metal that got knocked off inside the tank.

Mark 3ll; tank no. 799
captured near Arras,
France, on April 11, 1917

Renault FT tanks being operated by
the U.S. Army in France; Light tanks
with a crew of only two, these were
mass-produced during World War I

CHER AMI

German unmanned camera pigeon used for aerial reconnaissance in WWI

British soldiers sending out a carrier pigeon

On October 3, 1918, a group of American soldiers were trapped behind enemy lines. Their food and ammunition were gone, and more than 200 of them had already been killed. Just 194 men remained from the 500 who had started the battle.

The Germans kept firing at the men. They had food and ammunition. All they had to do was to wait and eventually they would be able to capture or kill the Americans. Major Charles Whittlesey knew things were desperate, so he called for one of the three homing pigeons.

During WWI, wireless radios were not reliable, so homing pigeons were used by the military to send messages back to headquarters. Through natural instinct, the pigeons would always return to their loft. They were so accurate that the messages got through 95% of the time.

Major Whittlesey wrote a note calling for reinforcements and stuffed the note into the small metal canister attached to the bird's leg. Then he released the pigeon. It was immediately shot down by the Germans. He called for the second pigeon, wrote another note, and released the bird. It too was killed.

They had one bird left. A pigeon named Cher Ami (French for "dear friend"), this pigeon was their last hope. The Major wrote a third note, put it in the silver cylinder, and released Cher Ami to the sky. He too was shot down.

But what the soldiers did not realize was that Cher Ami managed to get himself back into the air. Shot through the chest and blind in one eye, Cher Ami flew the 25 miles back to headquarters in just 65 minutes. When he arrived, his leg was hanging by just a tendon and he was covered in blood, but he delivered the message.

Reinforcement troops were immediately sent and the 194 men were rescued. Meanwhile, Army medics worked frantically to save Cher Ami's life. They had to amputate his leg, but he did recover. The medics carved him a little wooden leg and Cher Ami was awarded the French "Croix de guerre with avec palme" for heroic service. When the war was over, Cher Ami was sent home to live out the rest of his days in peace in the United States. When Cher Ami died, his body was preserved and put on display at the Smithsonian institute.

Thousands of pigeons like Cher Ami were used in WWI. The new "wireless" radios were unreliable and often broke down. Telegraph lines could be cut by the enemies, but the pigeons were fast and usually difficult to shoot.

Troops brought their pigeon lofts with them onto the battlefield. As they moved, they released the pigeons with messages to update headquarters on their progress. The birds had the amazing ability to find their way back to their loft deliver the message.

Both the Allies and the Central Powers used pigeons as messengers and both sides tried to shoot down and kill the other's messengers. Because the pigeons were so swift, they were difficult to kill, so soldiers brought in hawks to attack the pigeons. Even with the hawk attacks, the pigeons were the most reliable form of communication.

Most Valuable Bird: Pigeons

Pigeon lofts were carried to the front in a variety of ways. Some were carried on double-decker busses and others were packed in on the backs of soldiers. Homing pigeons were so important to the war effort that killing or wounding a pigeon was against the law and would get you 6 months in jail.

FLAMETHROWERS

The trenches were horrible. When it rained, they filled with mud, so the soldiers were ankle deep in water and slime. When it was dry, they were full of rats. And there were always, always fleas and lice. When men were killed, there was no place to bury them, so sometimes corpses were left on the ground to rot. It was a ghastly place.

Trench warfare became a standard part of World War I. The soldiers on both sides dug deep ditches in the ground so that they could hide behind the earthen walls and shoot at their enemies. The Allies dug temporary trenches that were cramped and narrow. The Germans, however, made strong deep trenches with bunkers that had planks to keep the men out of the mud. Some even had sleeping quarters for the officers.

But even the best trenches were atrocious places to live and work. The soldiers were stuck in the trenches fighting for months. Neither side was able to gain the advantage and move forward. Both sides became desperate for a way to force the other out of the trenches. If they could just get the men out of the trenches, then maybe they could end the war.

The Germans came up with a secret weapon that they were sure would drive the Allies above ground, and they used it for the first time to attack the British forces in July of 1915.

It was a typical afternoon for the British soldiers. They were sweltering under the intense heat of the July sun with no shade to be found. Some men were keeping watch in no man's land while others tried to rest. Suddenly, a wall of fire rolled over the trenches. Soldiers who saw it coming ran away in horror. Those who didn't were killed in a blast of flame. Terrified soldiers scrambled to get away from the flames. The trenches were burning, and there was nowhere to go but up. They scrambled out of the trenches, only to be met with enemy gunfire. The Allies had just met the German secret weapon: the flamethrower.

The Germans had strapped gas cylinders to their backs. A soldier with a fire-lit nozzle sprayed the gas and flame mixture over the trenches while fellow soldiers waited ready to shoot the men who fled the trenches. It was a terrible weapon, and in 2 days of fighting, the British forces lost more than 750 men.

The German army was sure its secret weapon was a success and fully expected to be able to drive the Allies out of the trenches with the threat of burning alive. But the Allies quickly learned that the soldier carrying the tanks of gas was the weakest link. Snipers became adept at aiming at the tanks and the soldiers operating the flamethrowers had a very short life expectancy.

In addition to being the target of the enemy, the soldier who was the flamethrower also had to deal with the possibility of the gas tanks exploding on their own. Being a flamethrower was considered the most dangerous job in the German Army.

Of course, once flamethrowing was introduced, the Allies also tried their hand at building portable fire devices. But they ran into the same problems as the Germans—with their flamethrowers being the target of snipers.

In the end, the flamethrowers were somewhat effective in moving men out of the trenches at a local level, but they were not nearly as effective as the Germans had hoped.

War Underground

Military leaders were desperate to find some way to move their enemies out of the trenches. One idea was to go underground. Miners were called in to dig tunnels deep under the trenches and load them with explosives. The idea was to blow the enemy out of the way. During the war they laid 958,000 pounds of explosives. The largest explosion could be heard more than 150 miles away.

POISON GAS

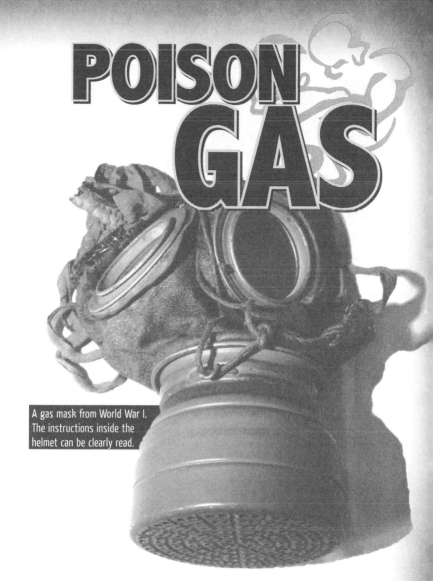

A gas mask from World War I. The instructions inside the helmet can be clearly read.

The soldier held the periscope up so he could see above the bank of the dirt trench. He peered out into no man's land looking for snipers or any sign of war activity. All was quiet except for a cloud on the horizon. The soldier rubbed his eyes and looked again. The cloud was a strange greenish-yellow. He lowered the periscope and shouted the alarm.

"Gas masks! Put on your gas masks!"

Americans wearing gas masks during World War I

Soldiers scrambled in the trenches, grabbing cloth gasmasks and putting them over their heads. Nobody wanted to be caught in the choking, horrible gas. And they never knew exactly what gas was being used. It could be blister-causing mustard gas or it might be deadly chlorine. The gas was heavier than air, so when it was released it sank into the trenches and was efficient in its killing.

The Germans were the first to use lethal gas in January of 1915. Warfare with deadly gasses had been banned by the Hague treaty, but the Germans believed the gas was an effective way of driving their enemies out of the trenches and decided to try it. The Allies were shocked and protested but the Germans refused to stop. So the Allies quickly armed their soldiers with gas masks and began shooting their own shells of killer gas. Many people died from inhaling the gas and some were blinded. Soldiers called it "a horrible weapon."

As the war went on, both armies built better gas masks. Chlorine could be rendered ineffective with a wet cloth over the mouth. So the armies started producing phosgene. Phosgene gas was quite deadly, but it didn't take effect immediately. A person could breathe in phosgene and still be able to fight for hours. Later he would become sick and die, but it didn't have the immediate effect that the military wanted.

Mustard gas was probably the most effective gas. It was not always fatal, but it caused blisters to form on the soldier's body, eyes, and inside the bronchial tubes. Soldiers could not fight after a mustard gas attack. The gas also polluted the ground where it was dropped. The oily gas sank to the ground and stayed in the soil for days.

Both sides used the poisonous gases, injuring an estimated 1.3 million people.

Nurse and author Vera Brittain wrote about her experience treating the soldiers in World War I affected by the poison gas:

> I wish those people who talk about going on with this war whatever it costs could see the soldiers suffering from mustard gas poisoning. Great mustard-coloured blisters, blind eyes, all sticky and stuck together, always fighting for breath, with voices a mere whisper, saying that their throats are closing and they know they will choke.

After World War I, most countries signed the Geneva Protocol, which states that the use of poisonous gas is condemned by the general opinion of the civilized world.

Pee in Your Socks!

That was the advice given to soldiers when they first started to encounter attacks of poison gas. Gas masks had not yet been invented, but scientists knew that chlorine reacted with the chemical urea, found in urine, and helped neutralize the gas. Holding pee-drenched socks over your nose and mouth could save your life. Everyone was happy when the first gas masks were invented in 1915.

ZEPPELINS

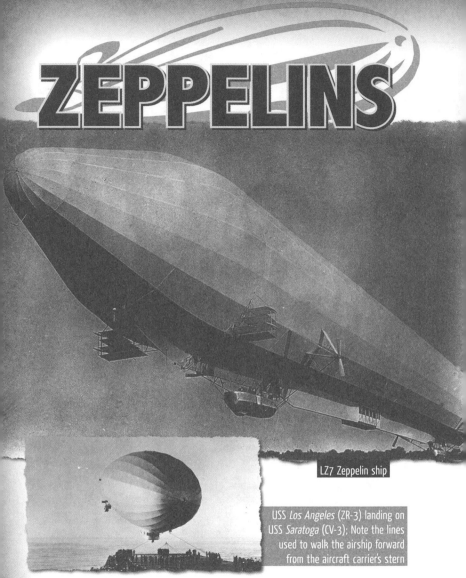

LZ7 Zeppelin ship

USS *Los Angeles* (ZR-3) landing on USS *Saratoga* (CV-3); Note the lines used to walk the airship forward from the aircraft carrier's stern

Flying high in the British night skies, the German Zeppelin was a silent enemy. Stashed in the Zeppelin were bombs ready to be dropped on London. The potential for a bombing raid terrified the British, who were not used to civilians being attacked during a war.

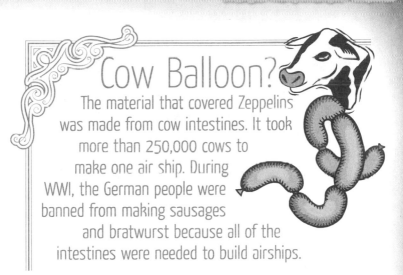

Cow Balloon?

The material that covered Zeppelins was made from cow intestines. It took more than 250,000 cows to make one air ship. During WWI, the German people were banned from making sausages and bratwurst because all of the intestines were needed to build airships.

The Germans had developed successful lighter-than-air flying machines in the 1890s. The huge, balloon-like ships were inflated with hydrogen gas and could fly hundreds of miles. Before the beginning of the war, Germany had been using Zeppelins as passenger air ships. But when the war began, military officers began to imagine ways to use the huge ships to fight in the war.

The first Zeppelin bombings were carried out as early as 1914, but the Germans learned that the ships could easily be shot down by land guns if they flew too low. The Germans developed Zeppelins that could fly higher and avoid being hit by land guns. They dropped artillery shells on London and Paris, causing damage to buildings and several casualties. The number of deaths was not high, but the emotional toll was incredible. People were terrified of the silent menace that could attack them at night without any warning.

The Allies knew they had to do something to protect their people. Their solution was to develop better airplanes that could fly higher and shoot the Zeppelins. This was quite effective. Once the air bag was punctured by the gunfire, the Zeppelin would often burst into flames.

People watching the landing of Zeppelin LZ 127

The Zeppelin bomb raids continued to torture the British and French throughout the war, but the Allies were increasing in their ability to shoot down the massive balloons. During the last year of the war, the Germans Zeppelins only went out on four bombing missions. During the war, the Germans built 84 Zeppelins—60 of which were lost to accidents and enemy action.

Want more perspective on what the Zeppelin bombings meant to the people of London and the race to find a way to neutralize the Zeppelins' threat? Watch an episode of *Nova* exploring the Zeppelins here: http://www.pbs.org/wgbh/nova/military/zeppelin-terror-attack.html

SPY TRAINING

Zeppelin Race

Zeppelins were filled with hydrogen gas to make them lighter than air. You can make a model of a Zeppelin with regular air and hold a Zeppelin race.

Materials:

- ❑ 2 long balloons
- ❑ 2 pieces of string cut to the same length
- ❑ Masking tape
- ❑ 2 plastic straws (do not use the bendable kind or cut off that part of the straw)
- ❑ Three friends and yourself

Divide into two racing teams. Each team member will hold one end of the "racing string" during the race. To prepare for the race, slide the string through the straw.

Then inflate the balloon as full as you can but don't tie it. Tape the straw to the top of the balloon. Then launch your Zeppelin and watch it fly. After you practice a few times, you will be ready to race against the other team.

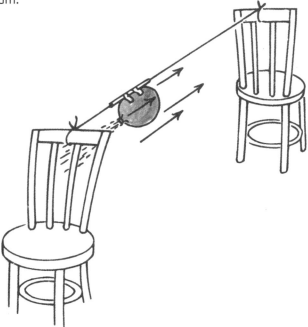

Periscope Up

German
U-boats
used
periscopes
to see
above the
water, but a periscope can also be used on land to peer
over walls and around corners. You can build your own
periscope with some easy-to-find materials.

Materials:

- ❏ 2 half-gallon juice
  or milk cartons
- ❏ 2 small square
  mirrors
- ❏ Scissors
- ❏ Tape

Construction Instructions:

1. Open the tops of both cartons and tape the open
   parts of the cartons together. This will make one
   long box.

2. Cut a flap on the opposite ends and sides of your long box. The flap should be the same height as your mirrors.
3. Tape a mirror to the inside of each flap.
4. Angle both mirror flaps inward. Look in the bottom of the periscope to see if you can see what is above. What you see in the top mirror should be reflected on the bottom mirror. Adjust your mirrors until you are happy with the angle.
5. Then tape the mirrors in place.
6. Begin spy practice with your new periscope.

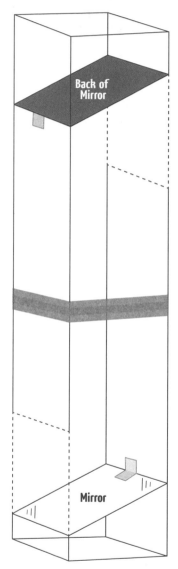

DOUGHBOYS
THE ALLIES' SECRET WEAPON

Wartime era portrait of a typical American doughboy, Hugh A. Ball, 1918

The Allies of Europe were counting on a secret weapon to end the war. It was a weapon that had the ability to produce guns and ammunition, could sail across oceans, and fight day and night. What was this amazing weapon? It was the fighting forces of the United States of America—otherwise known as the Doughboys.

The Germans were not afraid of the Americans entering the war. Kaiser Wilhelm II said it did not matter if the United States entered the war because they were "just a bunch of cowboys with an army barely worthy of the name."

But the Allied forces of Britain and France welcomed the Americans and affectionately called them the fighting Yanks,

Sammies, and Doughboys. It was the Doughboy nickname that stuck.

There are many theories as to why the Americans were called Doughboys. It was a nickname used during the Mexican-American War. Some historians say it was because as the American soldiers marched through the dry desert, they became covered with white dust and looked like they were made of dough. Others believe it was because of the American field rations of flour and rice that the soldiers had to mix up before they could eat it. Whatever the origin of the name, during World War I, it came to define the hard-working, hard-fighting American soldier.

In April of 1918, the American Army consisted of around 140,000 men, but after war was declared, the Army swelled in numbers. By August of 1918, America had sent more than 500,000 men to fight the Central Powers. Along with them came guns, trucks, ammunition, and supplies.

The Germans were stunned. They could not believe the numbers of fighters that were flooding the battlefields or the strength in the men fighting. Crown Prince Rupert of Bavaria complained, "The Americans are multiplying in a way we never dreamt of."

The fresh troops, guns, and ammunition from America propelled the Allies to victory, and in 1918, on the 11th day of the 11th month at 11:00 a.m., peace was declared. Today, November 11 is still remembered and celebrated as Veteran's Day.

U.S. 1st Infantry Division Doughboy as he would have looked in November 1918 during the Meuse-Argonne Offensive

SHARPSHOOTING HERO

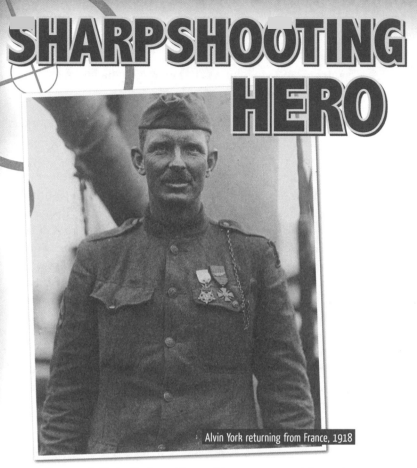

Alvin York returning from France, 1918

Corporal Alvin York and his soldiers were tired from the battle they had just fought. They had captured Hill 223 back from the Germans and were told to march forward through the French valley to the next mission. But as soon as the soldiers reached the open area, they were attacked from the hills above by machine gunfire.

The Allied soldiers were being mowed down by the zipping bullets. Men were being wounded in enormous numbers. Sergeant Bernard Early decided he had to lead a team to eliminate the machine guns or the entire platoon would be killed. He selected 17 men, including the sharpshooting Corporal York, and they set off for the machine gun nest.

Corporal York was used to hiding in the brush and tracking animals. Growing up in Tennessee, he had been an avid hunter and had helped feed his 10 brothers and sisters with the game he shot.

As a youth, he had been considered wild and had gotten in trouble for drinking and bar fighting. One of his friends was killed in a bar fight, and York decided he needed to clean up his act. He joined a church and became a dedicated member, often leading the congregation in singing.

York's church was against war, and when he was drafted, he wrote on his draft card, "Don't want to fight." He was denied status as a conscientious objector and was sent to train with the 82nd infantry division in Georgia. He was an excellent marksman and highly valued as a trained shooter, but he still did not want to fight.

Two of his commanders had long talks with him, pointing out Bible passages that showed that sometimes there was justification for war. York agreed to fight and was sent to Europe. That was how he found himself creeping from bush to bush, dodging machine gunfire, and looking for the German snipers.

As they crept through the brush, York and the men came upon hidden German headquarters. They took the officers as prisoners, but the machine guns began firing again.

Six of the men were killed, including York's commanding officer. Three more men were seriously wounded. This left York as the officer in charge. York commanded the remaining men to guard the prisoners, and York left to try to take out the machine gunners.

He sighted his gun and began to pick off the German gunners just like he had picked off birds when he was a boy in Tennessee. Suddenly, six German soldiers ran out of a trench and attacked York with bayonets. York drew his pistol and dropped all six before they could reach him.

He then switched back to his rifle and attacked the German machine gunners. When he had taken out about 20 soldiers, York began calling for the gunners to surrender. He didn't want to hurt any more than necessary.

A German major who had been captured by York's men agreed to the surrender and yelled to the men in German to lay down their weapons. York and his men rounded up the rest of the Germans and took them prisoner. They led their captives to battalion headquarters. York and his seven men had captured 132 prisoners and 35 machine guns. This was one of the most amazing captures of the war.

For his service, York was promoted to sergeant and awarded the Distinguished Service Cross, the Medal of Honor, the French Croix de guerre, and Italian Croce di Guerra. When he came home from the war, York was hailed as a hero and given a ticker tape parade in New York City.

York did not like this newfound fame and left New York as quickly as possible to return home to his beloved Tennessee. He married his sweetheart, Gracie Williams, and together they had seven children.

Hollywood filmmakers desperately wanted to make a movie about York's adventures in the war, but the modest York refused until 1941. When he finally agreed, the movie starred famous actor Gary Cooper and won an Academy Award.

York lived a quiet life in Tennessee and worked hard to improve educational opportunities for children in his home state. He was thrilled when the state opened the Alvin C. York Agricultural Institute. He died in 1954 at the age of 67 and was buried in his hometown of Pall Mall, TN.

HARLEM HELLFIGHTERS

New York's famous 369th regiment arrives home from France

Famous New York soldiers return home

Children gather along the line of the parade

Stones and dirt flew through the air as artillery shells pounded the ground. Flashes of fire lit up the night and the sound of guns and bombs pounded the air. Henry Johnson and Needham Roberts were standing watch for their unit when a grenade landed in their trench.

Sergeant Henry Lincoln Johnson, 369th Infantry ("Harlem Hellfighters"), in 1919, after receiving the French Croix de guerre

The explosion wounded Roberts and left Johnson alone to fight off the German patrol. Johnson grabbed his rifle and began shooting at the enemy soldiers. He spent his round, but there were more soldiers coming to attack his unit. Roberts unsheathed his bolo knife, turned his gun around—ready to use the butt of it as a club—and dove in to fight off 24 enemy soldiers.

It was actions of courage like this that earned the 369th Infantry the nickname "the Harlem Hellfighters." They were the first all-Black fighting unit to arrive in France and became the most decorated American regiment in World War I.

In the early 1900s, segregation was a significant problem in the United States. During World War I, White American soldiers and Black American soldiers were assigned to completely separate regiments and were not allowed to share the same quarters, train together, or fight together. This angered Black Americans, but many of them felt that serving in the military would prove the bravery and competence of Black Americans.

The German soldiers immediately recognized their tough fighting skills and started calling them the Höllenkämpfer or Hellfighters. The Hellfighters spent 191 days in front line trenches, longer than any other American unit. During this time, they never had any of their men captured and they never lost any ground. At the end of the war, 171 members of the 369th Infantry were awarded the Legion of Honor or the Croix de guerre.

FLYING *Spies*

Royal Aircraft Factory B.E.2c of the Royal Flying Corps in 1916

Airplanes were not much more than wire, canvas, and strings when the war began in 1914. The Wright brothers had just flown for the very first time in 1903. The start of WWI was only 5 short years since the first airplane had managed to make it across the English Channel. But military officers knew that this newfangled invention could be of great use as a tool for spying.

In earlier wars, military leaders had tried using balloons to spy on enemy troops to learn which direction they were moving and how many soldiers they had on the ground. The balloons were helpful, but they were easy to shoot down and difficult to control. Their effectiveness as a spy tool was limited.

But airplanes showed real promise for spying. Airplanes could fly higher and faster than balloons, plus in the hands of a good aviator, they had great maneuverability. From the very beginning of the war, both sides used airplanes to fly over enemy territory to spy on troop movements.

One of the first big battles was at Mons, in southern Belgium. The British had a two-seated biplane flying above the battleground. From their bird's-eye view, the observa-

Barking Airplanes?

The term "dogfight" originated during WWI. Fighter planes would turn off their engines in midair, while taking sharp twists and turns just so the engines wouldn't stall. When they started the engines back up, the plane would make a noise that sounded like dogs barking. That's why fighting planes became known as "dogfights."

tion team could see that the Germans were moving troops so that they could surround and attack the unsuspecting Allies. The warning from the observation team allowed the Allies to retreat and saved the lives of countless soldiers. Just a few days later, information from French aerial observers gave the Allies the advantage in the Battle of the Marne and saved Paris from invasion.

The airplane had proven itself as an important spy tool, and pilots from both the Allies and the Central Powers were given the job of flying reconnaissance missions and bringing back all of the information they could see.

Of course, that was also a big problem. Neither the Allies nor the Central Powers wanted planes flying over their camps, spying on their movements. The solution was for the pilots to arm themselves and if they saw an enemy plane, they would shoot at the pilot and try to take down the plane so the information would not get back to headquarters.

At first, the pilots just carried pistols. They would try to fly in close and shoot down the plane. The pilots became like cowboys of the Wild West, only instead of riding horses and shooting at each other, they were flying planes and shooting at each other. But soon pilots started mounting machine guns on their planes. Two-seated planes would have the machine gun mounted in the rear to defend the plane. Planes with the engine and propeller in the back could mount the machine gun on the front of the plane. But a plane with a propeller in the front was difficult to defend. The machine gun had to be mounted at an angle, so it would not shoot up the propeller of its own plane.

French pilot Roland Garros was the first aviator to use a machine gun that fired through the propeller. He worked with his mechanic to design tapered wedges of armor plate that were fitted to the inside faces of the propeller blades. The plates would deflect any bullets that might hit the blades when the machine gun was fired. This was only somewhat effective because the propeller blades were frequently damaged and they threw the engine out of alignment.

But when the machine gun worked, it was quite effective. In the first few weeks of April 1915, Garros shot down at least three enemy aircraft. Garros became a national hero in France and a wanted man in Germany.

Garros's luck ran out on April 19. His plane malfunctioned, and he was forced to land in enemy territory. He tried

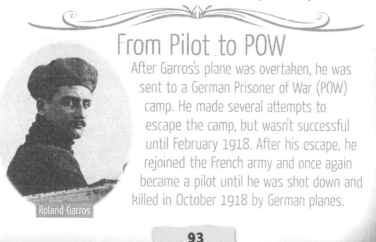

From Pilot to POW

After Garros's plane was overtaken, he was sent to a German Prisoner of War (POW) camp. He made several attempts to escape the camp, but wasn't successful until February 1918. After his escape, he rejoined the French army and once again became a pilot until he was shot down and killed in October 1918 by German planes.

Roland Garros

to destroy his plane so the Germans would not be able to see how his machine gun and propeller worked, but he was captured before he could get rid of the evidence.

The Germans immediately summoned airplane manufacturer Anthony Fokker to look at Garros's plane. Fokker was given 48 hours to duplicate the French machine gun and demonstrate it to the Germans.

Fokker and his team of engineers looked at Garros's invention and knew they could do better. They invented a machine gun whose rate of fire was regulated by the movement of the propeller. A cam in the engine prevented the gun from firing when the blades of the propeller were directly in line with the muzzle of the gun.

The Germans were amazed at Fokker's solution and wanted him to demonstrate how it would work on the battlefield. They ordered the aircraft builder to go up in the plane and shoot down a French pilot. Fokker went up, but he did not want to do any shooting. He decided to defy the Germans and landed the plane without taking a shot. He told the Germans he had done what they had asked by modifying the gun and engine, but they would have to do their own killing.

The German generals ordered one of their own pilots into the air and he came back triumphant, telling how well the gun worked. The Germans ordered Fokker's new weapon to be put on as many German planes as possible.

Immediately the Germans gained superiority in the air. Their machine guns could rip through the canvas and wood airplanes and sent many Allied pilots to their death. The Allies quickly countered and built their own interrupter machine gun. It was the start of the aerial dogfights, where pilots would hunt down pilots in order to keep them from spying on their territory.

It was a battle that made heroes out of young pilots and made Ace fighter pilots famous on both sides of the war.

The Real
RED BARON

The most famous of the flying Ace pilots was a young German officer named Manfred von Richthofen. Known for his red Fokker triplane, Richthofen was credited with shooting down 80 enemy aircraft. That was five more victories than any other pilot in the war.

As a young boy, Richthofen enjoyed playing outdoors, hiking, and competing in sports. Born into a wealthy family, he was expected to follow in the footsteps of his father and serve in the military, so at the age of 11 he was enrolled in the Cadet Corps. He hated it.

The teachers at the Cadet Corps were strict and demanding. Richthofen rebelled by refusing to do his schoolwork and often completed just enough to get by. He still liked playing games and sports, especially gymnastics and horseback riding. He won prizes for his feats on the horizontal bar.

When Richthofen graduated from military school, he joined a cavalry unit and served under Emperor Alexander III of the Russian Uhlan Regiment. He was still serving in the cavalry when war broke out. At first, he worked in reconnais-

Manfred von Richthofen, 1917

sance, getting and sending information for the officers. But when the trench warfare began, it was impossible for horses to get through the lines or even to walk in the muck and mud. The cavalry was disbanded and Richthofen was ordered to work for the army's supply branch. He hated it.

He wrote a letter to his commanding officer asking to be transferred to a unit where he could be of more use than counting bullets and peeling potatoes. He was given the opportunity to train as an observer with the Imperial German Army Air Service. In his biography, Richthofen wrote about the first time he went up in an airplane: "It was a glorious feeling to be so high above the earth, to be master of the air. I didn't care a bit where I was, and I felt extremely sad when my pilot thought it was time to go down again."

For a few months, Richthofen worked as an observer, flying high over Allied territory, taking pictures of enemy troops, and reporting his observations. But the more he was in the air, the more he wanted to learn to be a pilot. Finally, in October of 1915, he was sent to the Western front to learn to fly airplanes. He loved it.

In March of 1916, Richthofen was assigned his first aircraft—an Albatross C.III. He wrecked it on his very first flight. Amazingly, the military assigned him another plane and he began to prove his worth as a pilot.

Early in the fall of 1916, Ace fighter pilot Oswald Boelcke invited Richthofen to join his newly formed Jagdstaffel (fighter squadron). Richthofen was thrilled to be noticed by the famous aviator and immediately agreed to serve with him.

On September 17, just a few days after joining the fighter squadron, Richthofen shot down his first enemy plane. After his first victory was confirmed by military officials, Richthofen contracted a jeweler in Berlin to make him a silver cup. He had the cup engraved with the date and the type of enemy aircraft he had shot down. He added 60 cups to his collection and would have had 20 more made, but there was a shortage of silver due to the war, so the jeweler could no longer meet his orders.

Legends and stories about Richthofen claim that he was a daredevil reckless pilot that flew alone, hunting down enemy pilots. This was not the truth. In reality, he was a careful pilot who strategically planned his attacks. He almost always attacked by diving on an enemy aircraft with the sun behind his back. This gave him both a height and visual advantage. And when he was attacking, Richthofen fully expected that his fellow airmen would protect his rear and sides.

Another myth is that Richthofen always flew a Fokker triplane, but in truth, only 19 of his victories were in the Fokker. Most of the time he flew either an Albatros D.II or Albatros D.III.

After his 17th victory, Richthofen painted his Albatross a bright red. He wanted to be noticed by the other fliers. He also wanted them to be a bit afraid of the man in the bright red plane. It worked. It was rumored that the British put a price on the head of the pilot who flew the bright red plane. But even with a bounty on his head, Richthofen continued to shoot down his enemies. The other pilots both respected and feared him and began calling him Der rote Kampfflieger (The Red Battle Flier).

He became a national war hero with postcards that bore his picture. The Germans were proud of their flying ace and the German government wanted to keep him alive. As long as The Red Battle Flier was in the skies, the German people had hope. So in May 1917, Richthofen was ordered to take time off.

As a hero, he was expected to appear in public and rally the people for the war effort. He spoke to youth groups, was a guest of Kaiser Wilhelm II, and visited with many top generals. He was also allowed to go home and visit his mother. Additionally, he was asked to write his memoir so it could be published and would inspire more German enthusiasm for the war.

After a month of leave, Richthofen was back in his plane, and this time he was the commander of Jagdgeschwader I (Fighter Wing 1). Both Richthofen and his squadron were doing well until July 6, when Richthofen was hit in the head during air battle. For a moment he was blinded and his plane dove down, but his vision cleared somewhat and he managed to land his plane in friendly territory. It took several surgeries to remove all of the bone splinters from the wound, but Richthofen was back in his plane just 19 days after the accident (against his doctor's orders). It is believed that the injury caused lasting damage. He suffered from postflight nausea and headaches, and many people said he had a change in temperament or personality.

While he was on medical leave, German officials tried to talk him into taking job that would be safer, but Richthofen refused. German officials were dismayed. They did not want their national hero to be killed. It would be a great blow to national pride, but Richthofen said his place was in his airplane.

He returned to flying at the end of October 1917 and continued to fly through the winter and into the spring of 1918. But on April 21, 1918, while he was chasing a Canadian pilot in a Sopwith Camel, Richthofen was fatally shot in the chest. Before he died, he was able to land his plane without crashing. He landed in a territory that was controlled by Australian Imperial Forces.

Australian soldiers who ran to the aircraft reported that Richthofen was still alive when he landed, but died moments later. The Australians gave him a burial with full military honors. There is still a controversy about who actually killed him.

Top Ten Aces of WORLD WAR I

Pilot	Country/ Air Force	Victories
Manfred von Richthofen	Germany (Luftstreikräfte)	80 victories
René Fonck	France (Aéronautique Militaire)	75 victories
Billy Bishop	Canada (Royal Air Force)	72 vistories
Ernst Udet	Germany (Luftstreitkräfte)	62 victories
Edward Mannock	United Kingdom (Royal Air Force)	61 victories
Raymond Collishaw	Canada (Royal Air Force)	60 victories
James McCudden	United Kingdom (Royal Air Force)	57 victories
Andrew Beauchamp-Proctor	South Africa (Royal Air Force)	54 victories
Erich Löwenhardt	Germany (Luftstreitkräftc)	54 victories
Donald MacLaren	Canada (Royal Air Force)	54 victories

At first, it was thought that one of the Canadian pilots shot him, but later forensic analysis showed that the bullet probably came from a machine gun on the ground. We may never know for sure who brought down the greatest flying ace of World War I.

THE BLACK
Swallow
OF DEATH
FIRST BLACK AMERICAN FIGHTER PILOT

Corporal Eugene J. Bullard

It was dark in the hull of the ship—dark, smelly, and lonely, especially for a 12-year-old boy. But Eugene Bullard was determined to leave America and make his way to France. His father had told him stories about France, where Black people were treated as equals. It would be a very different world than the Southern United States in the early 1900s.

Bullard's mother was a Creek Indian, and his father grew up on the French island of Martinique. During his short life, Bullard had already witnessed a great deal of violence directed against Black people and had watched a mob try to lynch his father. Bullard believed life would be better for him if he could just get to France.

The ship he stowed away on landed in Scotland—a long way away from France. Bullard went to work doing any job he could find. He worked as a boxer and eventually joined a vaudeville troop that was traveling to Paris. When he finally arrived, he fell in love with the city and made it his home.

But in 1914, war broke out. Bullard was determined to fight for his adopted country. He joined the Foreign Legion and became a machine gunner. Bullard was very good at his job and accurate in his shooting. His regiment earned the nickname "The Swallows of Death" because they would swoop into an area with their team of crack shots and successfully fight their enemy.

The battles were grueling and deadly. Nearly half of the men in Bullard's division were killed. Bullard was severely wounded in his leg and had to spend months recovering. Despite his injury, Bullard wanted to return to the fight. He volunteered to join the French Air Service as a gunner.

On May 5, 1917, Eugene Bullard received his pilot's license from the Aéro-Club de France. He was assigned to Escadrille N 93 of the Lafayette Flying Corps and began flying Nieuport and Spad airplanes. Before the war, these were some of the fastest racing planes. They were lightweight single-seat planes that had been fitted with guns. Bullard started flying solo and proved to be a good pilot as well as an excellent marksman. His fellow pilots nicknamed him "The Black Swallow of Death."

Bullard took part in 20 successful combat missions, sometimes flying with his pet monkey, Jimmy. He became the first Black American to serve as a fighter pilot. When the United States joined the war, Bullard volunteered to serve with the U.S. Air Service, but he was not allowed to be a pilot because he was Black.

After the war, Bullard received numerous awards for his bravery and actions in battle. He decided to stay in Paris and eventually became the owner of his own nightclub, "L'Escadrille," named after his days as a fighter pilot. He became friends with many famous musicians including Josephine Baker and Louis Armstrong.

When World War II broke out, Bullard again went to work for France, this time as a spy. Because he knew how to speak German, French, and English, he could listen in on the conversations of the people who visited his nightclub and report information back to the French military. Bullard eventually took up arms and fought with the 51st Infantry and was seriously injured. He decided to return to America and made his home in Harlem, NY.

Bullard never fully recovered from his war injury and lived a quiet life working as an elevator operator. He never received recognition from America for his accomplishments during his lifetime, but the French considered Bullard a national hero.

In 1954, the French government honored Bullard by selecting him to help rekindle the flame at the tomb of the unknown soldier under the Arc de Triomphe, and in 1959, he was made a knight (chevalier) of the Légion d'honneur.

Bullard died in 1961 at the age of 66 and was buried with full military honors in the French War Veterans' section of the Flushing Cemetery in New York.

In 1994, 33 years after his death, Eugene Bullard was finally recognized by his own country. He was posthumously commissioned as a Second Lieutenant in the United States Air Force. In 2006, a movie, *Flyboys*, was made about Bullard and his flying comrades.

Hell's HANDMAIDEN

Fighter ace William Avery "Billy" Bishop poses with his aircraft in August 1917; at the time of this photograph, Bishop had downed 37 German planes and had received the Victoria Cross for his solo attack on four German aircraft on June 2, 1917

In 1917, the average fighter pilot had a life expectancy of about 11 days. Billy Bishop was on day 4. He was flying fourth in a four-ship patrol. He followed the other Nieuport planes as they climbed above the misty clouds to an altitude of 9,000 feet. There in the clear sky flew three German Albatross planes.

Bishop's instinct kicked in and he dived toward the tail of the enemy plan and fired his gun. He saw the bullets hit the plane and the German pilot dived. Bishop stayed on his tail and followed the German through the clouds. Bishop suspected it could be a trick. The German pilot might be faking a

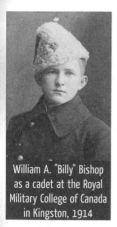

William A. "Billy" Bishop as a cadet at the Royal Military College of Canada in Kingston, 1914

crash and getting away only to come back and attack the other Allied pilots.

Bishop was right. Below the clouds the German leveled out his plane. Bishop took aim with his Lewis gun and blasted the plane near the fuselage. The German plane dove nose first and crashed into a field. Bishop had his first victory.

But seconds later, Bishop's excitement turned into terror. The engine of his own plane sputtered and died. Desperately, he tried to get the engine to restart, but it wouldn't turn over. Bishop was silently dropping to the ground. He aimed the nose of the Nieuport to what he hoped was friendly territory and bounced to a stop.

Machine gun fire was exploding around him. Bishop grabbed the only weapon he had—his flare gun—ran for the closest trench, and dove in. He had no idea if he had just entered an Allied trench or a German trench. Four men ran toward him and he aimed his flare gun but he didn't fire. To his relief, they had on British uniforms. Bishop had lived to fly another day.

During the next month, Billy Bishop managed to shoot down 20 enemy aircraft. He was such an excellent marksman that the Germans gave him the nickname "Hell's Handmaiden." They put a bounty on his head, and other German pilots actively hunted for him on their patrols. Shooting down Billy Bishop became the goal of the German pilots.

Born in Ontario, Canada, Billy Bishop enjoyed shooting, riding, and swimming. He was fascinated by the invention of the airplane and even tried to build his own out of cardboard, wire, and string. He launched it from the roof of his house. When he crashed, his younger sister dug him out of the wreckage. Billy was determined to fly one day and got his chance with the Royal Flying Corps.

No Parachute?

At the start of the war pilots were not given parachutes. Not because they hadn't been invented, they had! It was because military officials believed that if they had parachutes, the pilots would jump out at the first hint of danger and too many airplanes would be lost. What the officials didn't realize was that pilots were difficult to train and far more valuable than the aircraft. Parachutes were finally issued to pilots a year after the war ended.

As a pilot, Bishop was considered only average. He had a difficult time with landings and the "Bishop Landing" became a Flying Corps joke. But Bishop was an excellent marksman and had an amazing ability to manage the plane and the gun. He was given the assignment of flying "lone wolf" to hunt by himself for German airplanes.

By the middle of June 1918, Bishop had outlived many of his fellow pilots and had scored an amazing 67 victories. He was an international hero and the Allied leaders were afraid that if he were killed, it would have a terrible effect on the public morale. Bishop was given orders to return to England to help organize the Canadian Air Force.

Bishop was angry at being called off the field and wrote to his wife, "I've never been so furious in my life. It makes me livid with rage to be pulled away just as things are getting started."

He was scheduled to leave the French aerodrome at noon on June 19. He got up early that morning and took off in his plane. He was determined to have one last mission before he left the battlefield.

Dropping down through cloud cover, Bishop spotted three German Pfalz D.III scouts. These were tough German planes that were built to withstand a great deal of battle damage. These planes were deadly weapons, and they had spotted Bishop.

As they circled around to attack, Bishop sighted his gun. He got off shots as the three planes fired and dove beneath him. Bishop glanced behind his plane and saw two more German fighters headed toward him.

Bishop decided to follow the three original planes and dove down, firing and hitting one plane. It fell to the ground. The two new planes dove and shot at Bishop, but as he turned quickly and flew out of the way, the two German planes ran into each other and crashed. Bishop then took off after the two remaining planes. He managed to shoot one down but the other escaped. Bishop dropped his plane down to 900 feet and began to think about returning to the base, but then he saw the distant outline of another German plane. In the final fight, Bishop was the winner.

The last German plane went down, and Bishop was left alone in the sky. He returned back to his base ready to fulfill his duty and go to England. What he didn't realize was that he had set a record that morning by downing five enemy planes in only 15 minutes. He ended his career with an amazing record of 72 victories.

After the war, Bishop continued to work with aircraft and served as the chairman of British Airlines. When World War II started, Bishop was appointed to the post of Air Marshal of the Royal Canadian Air Force. He continued to work in the aeronautical field until he retired. Ace fighter pilot Billy Bishop died in Palm Beach, FL, at the age of 62. He definitely outlived the average fighter pilot's lifespan of 11 days.

SPY TRAINING

Battleship

You can learn how to think strategically just like the secret forces did in World War I. Practice by playing the paper and pencil game of Battleship.

Materials:

- ❑ Graph paper
- ❑ Pencil
- ❑ Friend to play against

Count off your graph paper and mark it into two 10 x 10 grids. Across the top, label the squares A–J. Down the side, label the squares 1–10. One grid should be labeled Self and the other Opponent.

Then each player secretly decides where they are going to place their ships: a five-space battleship, a four-space cruiser, a three-space submarine, and a two-space destroyer.

None of the ships may be placed diagonally; they must all be placed in straight lines either horizontally or vertically. The ships are marked by coloring in the appropriate spaces.

Players take turns taking shots at each other. A shot is taken by calling out the coordinates of a space on the 10 x 10 grid. Each player takes one shot at a time. If the player calls the coordinates of a space where a ship is located, her opponent tells her so by saying "hit." If she misses, her opponent says "miss."

Players should take care to mark the shots they take on their "Opponent" grid, and whether each shot was a hit or a miss, so that they don't call any space more than once. Players may also mark the "Self" grid with shots taken by their opponent.

A ship is sunk when all of its squares have been hit. When this happens, the player whose ship was sunk says, for example, "You sank my battleship." First person to sink all of his or her opponents' ships wins!

BATTLESHIP EXAMPLE

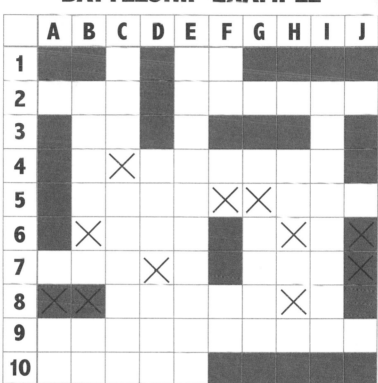

SPY TRAINING

Doughboy Cakes

The Doughboys and other soldiers often longed for a taste of home. In WWI, the American Red Cross came up with a recipe for a cake that would stay fresh for a long period of time and could be shipped to the soldiers serving in Europe. With help from your family, you can make a cake like one the Doughboys would have enjoyed.

Materials:

- ❑ Help from an adult
- ❑ 1 cup orange juice for soaking raisins
- ❑ 8 ounces raisins (about one package), chopped, soaked in orange juice, and drained before use
- ❑ 2 cups brown sugar
- ❑ 2 cups hot water
- ❑ 2 tablespoons lard (butter may be substituted today, but lard helped the cake stay fresher.)

- ❑ 1 teaspoon salt
- ❑ 1 teaspoon cinnamon
- ❑ 1 teaspoon cloves
- ❑ 4 ounces pecans or walnuts, chopped
- ❑ 1 tablespoon finely grated orange zest
- ❑ 3 cups flour
- ❑ 1 teaspoon baking soda

Female workers from the Salvation Army in helmets and carrying gas masks are making pies for soldiers in Ansonville, France

Soak chopped raisins in orange juice at least for a few hours, or up to one week. Drain. Preheat oven to 350°F.

Put raisins, sugar, hot water, lard, salt, cinnamon, cloves, nuts, and grated zest in a large pot. Bring to a boil over medium heat, stirring frequently, then reduce the heat to low and cook at a simmer for 5 minutes. Remove from heat and cool in a large bowl.

Sift or stir the flour and baking soda together, then add to liquid. Mix well.

Generously grease two small loaf pans or one tube pan. Pour batter into the pans and bake for 45 minutes or until a knife blade comes out clean when poked into the cake.

Doughnuts
for Doughboys

Soldiers on the front lines didn't just enjoy baked treats sent from home. On the battlefields of France, Salvation Army workers often served doughnuts and coffee to the men in the trenches. Why doughnuts? Because rations were so poor, The Salvation Army decided that the tasty treats would bring the men a bit of cheer as they ate something that reminded them of home and their families. However, because only limited resources were available to the volunteers on the front, the doughnuts had to be fried seven at a time, with some cleverly being cooked in soldier's helmets! Donut Day is still celebrated each year by The Salvation Army and its partners to remember the aid and comfort the volunteers gave the soldiers on the battlefield.

Recruits for U.S. Marine Corps being sworn in at recruiting station, New York City, 1918

BIBLIOGRAPHY

BOOKS

Atwood, K. J. (2014). *Women heroes of World War I: 16 remarkable resisters, soldiers, spies, and medics.* Chicago, IL: Chicago Review Press.

Bowen, E. (1980). *Knights of the air.* New York, NY: Time Life Books.

Clark, G. B. (1999). *Devil dogs: Fighting Marines of World War I.* New York, NY: Presidio Press.

Cook, A. (2002). *Ace of spies: The true story of Sidney Reilly.* Gloucestershire, England: The History Press.

Harris, C. H., & Sadler, L. R. (2003). *The archeologist was a spy: Sylvanus G. Morley and the Office of Naval Intelligence.* Albuquerque: University of New Mexico Press.

Heyman, N. M. (2002). *Daily life during World War I.* Westport, CT: Greenwood Press.

Kramer, A. (2011). *Women wartime spies.* New York, NY: MJF Books.

Livesey, A. (1989). *Great battles of World War I.* New York, NY: Macmillan.

Pincock, S. (2006). *Codebreaker: The history of codes and ciphers, from the ancient pharaohs to quantum cryptography.* New York, NY: Walker.

Shores, C. (2001). *British and empire aces of World War I.* Oxford, England: Osprey.

Ulanoff, S. (1975). *Illustrated history of World War I in the air.* New York, NY: Arco Publishing.

Willmott, H. P. (2004). *World War I.* New York, NY: DK.

WEBSITES

Allen, P. (2011). 'Second Paris' built towards end of First World War to fool Germans. *The Telegraph.* Retrieved from http://www.telegraph.co.uk/news/worldnews/europe/france/8879053/Second-Paris-built-towards-end-of-First-World-War-to-fool-Germans.html

American Red Cross. (n.d.). *Partnership with America's military members.* Retrieved from http://www.redcross.org/about-us/history/red-cross-american-history/military-partnership

Asantewaa, Y. (2014). The legendary 'Harlem Hellfighters'—As the Germans called them. *Patapaa.* Retrieved from http://patapaa.com/2014/04/26/the-legendary-harlem-hellfighters-as-the-germans-called-them/

Atwood, K. J. (2014). *Marthe Cnockaert: Belgian spy.* Retrieved from http://womenheroesofwwi.blogspot.com/2014/02/martha-cnockaert-belgian-spy.html

Bell, M. (2009). *The real James Bond.* Retrieved from https://suite.io/martin-bell/1s7r2y6

Bootie. (2012). *Pigeons* [forum post]. Retrieved from http://www.thefewgoodmen.com/thefgmforum/threads/pigeons.12020/

Chester, J. (2014). World War One: Scientist John Haldane tested gas on himself. *BBC News.* Retrieved from http://www.bbc.com/news/uk-england-oxfordshire-25843294

Clements, K. (2012). *The animals sent to war: the facts behind the fiction in 'War Horse.'* First World War Centenary, Imperial War Museum. Retrieved from http://www.1914.org/news/the-animals-sent-to-war-the-facts-behind-the-fiction-in-war-horse/

Cooper, R. (2013). Revealed: How Germans were banned from eating sausages during WWI because intestines of 250,000 cows were needed to make each Zeppelin. *Daily Mail.* Retrieved from http://www.dailymail.co.uk/news/article-2400890/Germans-banned-eating-sausages-World-War-One-intestines-250-000-cows-needed-make-Zeppelin-airship.html

Ensminger, J. (2011). *Messenger dogs: Soldiers in the Great War.* Retrieved from http://doglawreporter.blogspot.com/2011/06/messenger-dogs-soldiers-in-great-war.html

Garner, C. W. (n.d.). *Bullard, Eugene Jacques (1894–1961).* Retrieved from http://www.blackpast.org/aah/bullard-eugene-jacques-1894-1961

Greenhill, S. (2013). A soldier's best friend: Efforts of 20,000 dogs on the front line in World War I discovered in records that show they carried aid to the wounded and pulled equipment. *Daily Mail.* Retrieved from http://www.dailymail.co.uk/news/article-2514593/Efforts-20-000-dogs-line-World-War-I-discovered-records.html

GSCNC Girl Scout History Project. (2014). *Who's that Girl Scout? The peach pit girls.* Retrieved from http://gshistory.com/tag/peach-pits/

History.com. (n.d.). *Christmas truce of 1914.* Retrieved from http://www.history.com/topics/world-war-i/christmas-truce-of-1914

History Learning Site. (2005). *Pigeons and World War One.* Retrieved from http://www.historylearningsite.co.uk/pigeons_and_world_war_one.htm

History Learning Site. (2011). *Poison gas and World War One.* Retrieved from http://www.historylearningsite.co.uk/poison_gas_and_world_war_one.htm

Kostka, D. (2011). *Air reconnaissance in World War I.* Retrieved from http://www.militaryhistoryonline.com/wwi/articles/airreconinwwi.aspx

Krumboltz, M. (2011). During World War I, France built a fake Paris to fool Germany. *Yahoo News.* Retrieved from http://news.yahoo.com/blogs/upshot/during-world-war-france-built-fake-paris-fool-213735364.html

Lienhard, J. H. (n.d.). *No. 827: War zeppelins.* Retrieved from http://www.uh.edu/engines/epi827.htm

Mission Centenaire. (n.d.). *Fernand Jacopozzi, "Magician of the light."* Retrieved from http://centenaire.org/en/fernand-jacopozzi-magician-light

National Archives. (n.d.). *Teaching with documents: Photographs of the 369th Infantry and African Americans during World War I.* Retrieved from http://www.archives.gov/education/lessons/369th-infantry/

National Archives. (n.d.). *Teaching with documents: The Zimmermannn telegram.* Retrieved from http://www.archives.gov/education/lessons/Zimmermannn/

Noe, D. (n.d.). *Mata Hari.* Retrieved from http://www.mata-hari.com/mata-hari-en.html

Old Magazine Articles. (2008). *War stories of the W.W. I carrier pigeons.* Retrieved from http://www.oldmagazinearticles.com/WW1_carrier-pigeons_information

Ptak, J. F. (2010). *World War I images--Pigeons, dardenelles, map of the Belgian front, October 1915.* Retrieved from http://longstreet.typepad.com/books/2010/11/world-war-i-images-pigeons-dardenelles-map-of-the-belgian-front-october-1915.html

Ross, J. F. (2014). *Why pilots didn't wear parachutes during World War 1.* Retrieved from http://www.thehistory reader.com/modern-history/parachutes-world-war-1/

Sherman, S. (2012). *Manfred von Richthofen.* Retrieved from http://acepilots.com/wwi/ger_richthofen.html

Simanitis, D. (2014). *Celebrating Eugene Bullard.* Retrieved from http://simanaitissays.com/2014/02/19/celebrating-eugene-bullard/

SpyMuseum.com. (n.d.). *Sidney Reilly.* Retrieved from http://spymuseum.com/dt_portfolio/sidney-reilly/

Tanks Encyclopedia. (2011). *WWI British armor.* Retrieved from http://www.tanks-encyclopedia.com/ww1/gb/british_wwI_tanks.php

Tanks Encyclopedia. (2011). *Little Willie.* Retrieved from http://www.tanks-encyclopedia.com/ww1/gb/little_willie.php

Tarver, N. (2013). World War One: The circus animals that helped Britain. *BBC News.* Retrieved from http://www.bbc.com/news/uk-england-24745705

The Salvation Army. (2014). *The history of Donut Day.* Retrieved from http://www.salarmychicago.org/donut day/donutDayHistory.htm

Toronto Dreams Project. (2010). *Hell's Handmaiden gets hitched.* Retrieved from http://torontodreamsproject. blogspot.com/2010/09/hells-handmaiden-gets-married. html

Townsend, R. T. (2014). *Lewis machine gun in World War I.* Retrieved from http://www.digitalhistoryproject.com/2012/08/lewis-machine-gun-in-world-war-i.html

Uboat.net. (n.d.). *His Imperial German Majesty's U-boats in WWI.* Retrieved from http://www.uboat.net/history/wwi/part5.htm

Watson, L. (2013). The Army's special branch: How bizarre fake spy trees appeared in no-man's land during WWI (and killed hundreds of soldiers). *Daily Mail.* Retrieved from http://www.dailymail.co.uk/news/article-2274260/The-Armys-special-branch-How-bizarre-fake-spy-trees-appeared-mans-land-WWI.html

Wikipedia. (n.d.). *Chemical weapons in World War I.* Retrieved from http://en.wikipedia.org/wiki/Chemical_weapons_in_World_War_I

Wikipedia. (n.d.). *Q-ship.* Retrieved from http://en.wikipedia.org/wiki/Q-ship

Windsor, L. (n.d.). *Billy Bishop.* Retrieved from http://roadstories.ca/billy-bishop/

ABOUT THE AUTHOR

Stephanie Bearce is a writer, a teacher, and a history detective. She loves tracking down spies and uncovering secret missions from the comfort of her library in St. Charles, MO. When she isn't writing or teaching, Stephanie loves to travel the world and go on adventures with her husband, Darrell.

More Books in This Series

Stealthy spies, secret weapons, and special missions are just part of the mysteries uncovered when kids dare to take a peek at the *Top Secret Files*. Featuring books that focus on often unknown aspects of history, this series is sure to hook even the most reluctant readers, taking them on a journey as they try to unlock some of the secrets of our past.

Top Secret Files: The American Revolution

George Washington had his own secret agents, hired pirates to fight the British, and helped Congress smuggle weapons, but you won't learn that in your history books! Learn the true stories of the American Revolution and how spies used musket balls, books, and laundry to send messages. Discover the female Paul Revere, solve a spy puzzle, and make your own disappearing ink. It's all part of the true stories from the *Top Secret Files: The American Revolution*.

ISBN-13: 978-1-61821-247-4

Top Secret Files: The Civil War

The Pigpen Cipher, the Devil's Coffee Mill, and germ warfare were all a part of the Civil War, but you won't learn that in your history books! Discover the truth about Widow Greenhow's spy ring, how soldiers stole a locomotive, and the identity of the mysterious "Gray Ghost." Then learn how to build a model submarine and send secret light signals to your friends. It's all part of the true stories from the *Top Secret Files: The Civil War*.

ISBN-13: 978-1-61821-250-4

Top Secret Files: World War II

Spy school, poison pens, exploding muffins, and Night Witches were all a part of World War II, but you won't learn that in your history books! Crack open secret files and read about the mysterious Ghost Army, rat bombs, and doodlebugs. Discover famous spies like the White Mouse, super-agent Garbo, and baseball player and spy, Moe Berg. Then build your own secret agent kit and create a spy code. It's all part of the true stories from the *Top Secret Files: World War II*.

ISBN-13: 978-1-61821-244-3